Overcoming the Mother Wound

Overcoming the Mother Wound

A Transformative Journey of Healing and Empowerment

Mari Grande, LCSW, LCAT, ATR-BC

Overcoming the Mother Wound

Copyright © 2024 Creative Healing Integration, Inc.

All rights reserved.

Published by Red Penguin Books Bellerose Village, NY

Library of Congress Control Number: 2024904521

ISBN

Digital 978-1-63777-546-2

Print 978-1-63777-547-9

This book is meant for educational, informational, and demonstration purposes only and is not offering medical advice or medical treatment. The information it contains is not intended to be used for self-diagnosis or to replace medical care. Always consult qualified healthcare providers for advice on medical issues. The information found within does not create a therapeutic relationship or guarantee better mental health or physical movement. Neither the author nor the publisher assumes any liability for any adverse consequences that may result from the information and material presented in this book.

No part of this book may be reproduced in any form or by any electronic or mechanical means, including information storage and retrieval systems, without written permission from the author, except for the use of brief quotations in a book review.

The digital version of this book requires a separate journal and art materials to make use of its experiential learning style.

About the Cover –

The image of the Dahlia, which is also the logo for Creative Healing Integration, Inc., represents both strength and fragility. The Dahlia flower symbolizes courage, beauty, and the strength required to experience and invite in the healing powers available to you. It represents grace under pressure, inner strength, and the move toward major life changes.

Thank you to John Grande, my husband, for editing this glorious flower to match the vision of *Overcoming the Mother Wound*.

*May this book bring hope and inspiration
to those already on, or just beginning
a journey of growth and self expression.*

TABLE OF CONTENTS

PREFACE	**11**
INTRODUCTION	**15**
ASSESSMENT #1	20
ASSESSMENT #2	22
CHAPTER 1: SETTLING	**23**
A: SETTLING	24
B: SELF-REFLECTION; WHAT WE THINK EXERCISE	26
C: ART TIME	28
D: SUPPORT WORK	32
E: CONCLUSION	33
CHAPTER 2: ATTACHMENT STYLES	**35**
A: ATTACHMENT STYLES - CHILD	36
B: SUPPORTWORK	46
C: QUIZ	47
D: CONCLUSION	49
CHAPTER 3: RESOURCING	**51**
A: WHAT YOU NEED	52
B: ABOUT RESOURCING	55
C: MANDALA EXERCISE - WHAT YOU NEED - RESOURCE -	57
D: GUIDED MEDITATION: BEST SELF RESOURCE	60
E: SUPPORT STONES - RESOURCE	62
F: CONCLUSION & SUPPORT WORK	64

CHAPTER 4: PENDULATE — 67

- A: PENDULATION — 68
- B: WOT — 69
- C: UNSCRAMBLING EXERCISE — 71
- D: WHAT WE THINK — 79
- E: MEDITATION RESOURCE: CALM PLACE – GUIDED MEDITATION (GM) APPENDIX E — 82
- F: ART TIME - YOUR CALM PLACE ART MAKING EXPERIENCE — 86
- G: CONCLUSION & SUPPORTWORK — 87

CHAPTER 5: DIALOGUE WITH THE CRITIC — 89

- A: OVERVIEW — 90
- B: PART 1 - ART MAKING EXPERIENCE — 91
- C: PART 2 – WHO IS THE CRITIC — 93
- D: PART 3 - DIALOGUING — 95
- E: ART TIME 1: EXAGGERATE THE CRITIC — 96
- F: ART TIME 2: CONTAIN THE CRITIC — 98
- G: CONCLUSION & SUPPORT WORK — 99

CHAPTER 6: SELF-ACCEPTANCE AND RESOURCING — 101

- A: OVERVIEW & PRE-WORK — 102
- B: RESOURCING AND SELF-ACCEPTANCE — 106
- C: MEDITATION RESOURCE: YOUR ANIMAL (APPENDIX C) — 107
- D: MEET YOUR ANIMAL - JOURNALING AND ART-MAKING EXERCISE TO TAKE IT FURTHER — 109
- E: ART TIME: MEET YOUR ANIMAL — 111
- F: CONCLUSION & SUPPORT WORK — 112

CHAPTER 7: MOTHER WOUND – SOLAR PLEXUS CHAKRA — 115

- A: OVERVIEW & PRE-WORK — 116
- B: SUPPORT EXERCISES: — 117
- C: CHAKRAS — 118

D: EXPLORING THE MOTHER WOUND. THE SOLAR PLEXUS GUIDED MEDITATION (APPENDIX F)	120
E: ART TIME: SOLAR PLEXUS ART-MAKING EXPERIENCE	122
F: CONCLUSION & SUPPORT WORK	123

CHAPTER 8: TYPES OF MOTHER WOUND — **127**

A: OVERVIEW & PRE-WORK	128
B: SUPPORT EXERCISES:	130
C: GUIDED MEDITATION: TYPES OF MOTHER WOUNDS (APPENDIX G)	131
D: ART TIME: MOTHER WOUND JOURNALING AND ART-MAKING EXERCISE	137
E: MOTHER WOUNDS	138
F: MOTHER WOUNDS:	152
G: CONCLUSION & SUPPORT WORK	153

CHAPTER 9: GIFT OF THE CRITICAL MOTHER — **157**

A: OVERVIEW & PRE-WORK	158
B: ART MAKING: MOSAIC "GIFT OF THE CRITICAL MOTHER" EXERCISE, ORIGINALLY IN-VISIONED BY KARLA HANKES, PHD.	160
C: CONCLUSION & SUPPORT WORK	169

EPILOGUE — **171**

A: OVERVIEW & POST-WORK	172
B: PUTTING IT ALL TOGETHER	173
C: POST-COURSE QUESTIONNAIRE	174
D: MOTHER-CHILD DIALOGUE ART-MAKING AND JOURNALING EXERCISE.	177

ACKNOWLEDGEMENTS — **181**

APPENDIX A: ART MATERIALS	183
APPENDIX B: BOOK RECOMMENDATIONS	184
APPENDIX C: GUIDED MEDITATION - ANIMAL	186
APPENDIX D: GUIDED MEDITATION - BEST SELF	188
APPENDIX E: GUIDED MEDITATION - CALM PLACE	189

APPENDIX F: GUIDED MEDITATION - SOLAR PLEXUS	191
APPENDIX G: GUIDED MEDITATION - TYPES OF MOTHER WOUNDS	193
APPENDIX H: MOTHE WOUND ART PROMPT	199
APPENDIX I: MOTHER WOUND SELF-ASSESSMENT	200
APPENDIX J: ONLINE COURSE LINK	202
APPENDIX K: SELF-CARE SHEET	203
APPENDIX L: SETTLING EXERCISE	204
APPENDIX M: SETTING AN INTENTION	205
APPENDIX N: TREE OF STRENGTH	206
APPENDIX O: UNSCRAMBLE EXERCISE	208
REFERENCES	**209**
ABOUT THE AUTHOR	**211**
NOTES	**213**

PREFACE

Overcoming the
Mother Wound

Like the mother-child relationship of many other people, my relationship with my mother has always been one of intensity. My mother was my first love, the best version. I always felt a deep connection with her. As a child, I could tell her anything, and she was always there to listen. As I grew older, that connection became confusing and painful.

As my interests differed from hers, so did her interest in me. It became clear that what I once experienced as unconditional love and acceptance was conditioned on not being separate from her and her ideals. When I shared an emotion, it was dismissed, minimized, or criticized.

Both my parents had no interest in me dating. I would stay virginal until I met a nice Greek doctor or lawyer. (I'll save those stories for another book.) Suffice it to say I got too many mixed messages about what to do, and my overwhelm forced me to shut down deep inside.

I lost that precious bond that I had held onto for so many years with my mother. If I went to her, I would be criticized for being weak or stupid for liking a boy or thinking in a certain way. Or she would bring my father into the fray, where outside of the criticism, I would also be judged. This aloneness devastated my psyche. My confusion and distress became unbearable.

Instead of feeling, I was eating or obsessing about food. In order to regain control over my excesses, I begged to see a therapist. Although it was considered taboo in my family, I was taken to a psychiatrist (not a therapist) in 1970. I spent the session obsessing about what I ate and how that made me feel. (I developed an eating disorder). The doctor failed to hear my distress, told my mother I was fine, and dismissed my concerns as trivial. After all, I was not suicidal or homicidal, and I looked "regular."

When, years later, I felt my veil of gloom lifting, it was because of a combination of love and art. I fell in love at a time when I decided to pursue my love of drawing and painting. It was a time when I found inspiring teachers, mentors, and a warm, creative, intelligent therapist.

That was the start of many years of healing, heartache, and revelations stemming from what I now understand as a Mother Wound. This is a deep wound; it sets into one's being at a very early age. It is internal, emotional, and disorganizing.

As an adult, when I connected with a therapist on my own, there was no talk of a Mother Wound or Complex Post-Traumatic Syndrome Disorder or CPTSD.* In my studies to become a psychotherapist, I learned about developmental attachment, emotional wounds, and the meaning of CPTSD. I was admittedly obsessed with the mother/child dyad.

It wasn't until I was browsing the courses on the New Age OM website that I found the word "Mother Wound."

Then it all fell into place. A Mother Wound is a relational wound from childhood, a hurt that was repeated, ignored, or ridiculed. It is not a physical wound, but it can be felt physically.

As an art and trauma psychotherapist, I listen to men and women share their stories, patterns, and pain points. Often, they are struggling with a difficult relationship with their mothers. In an effort to help a client, I sought out a group for daughters of critical mothers. I was surprised to learn that no such group had formed in New York City—hadn't treatment for CPTSD become mainstream?

It became clear that there was a burning need, and I should start such a group. I asked my female clients if they were interested, and almost all were eager to join.

A powerful group of women formed, and the healing began. Over time, I decided to focus on *Overcoming the Mother Wound* and decided to bring male clients into the conversation. Men, too, had Mother Wounds; such wounds were not limited to one sex, sexual orientation, or gender identification.

Eventually, I wrote this book to help others. Living with a Mother Wound is a painful, confusing way to live your life. Through personal experience, study, extensive therapy, and life lessons, I now have the tools to help others who want to overcome a Mother Wound and enjoy the pleasures of self-confidence and emotional clarity.

1. Complex Post Traumatic Symptom Disorder is not recognized in the Diagnostic Statistical Manual (DSM), the standard guide for psychiatric diagnoses in the USA. Side note, the International Classification of Diseases (ICD-11) does include a diagnosis of CPTSD. This statement is important because as long as CPTSD is not recognized in the DSM, insurance companies will not recognize that diagnosis.

INTRODUCTION

Overcoming the
Mother Wound

What is a Mother Wound? Who gets one? How do you get one? How do you know if you have one? What are the symptoms? How do you heal it?

A Mother Wound is a relational wound, meaning it is a wound that developed from a relationship, or lack of one, when we most needed one. When our physical, spiritual, and emotional needs are not met, we develop what I call the Mother Wound. A mother, in this context, can be a biological or adoptive mother, a stepmother, or any person (related or not) who significantly impacts a child's well-being (i.e., physical, emotional, or spiritual).

A Mother Wound can cause low energy, lack of motivation, and self-doubt. Or it may cause trouble settling or finding calm throughout the day. It is a wound that develops at a young age through a mismatch of temperaments, a wound born out of neglect and cruelty, intentional or not. It is a wound that creates divisions inside of us.

If you or someone you know is struggling with a strong, critical voice that won't let up, believe that to overcome something, you must work harder and harder, believe you are doing it wrong or you do not deserve to get what you want or believe that what you have and who you are is not good enough, you are living with a Mother Wound. (Spoiler alert: we all have one—a Mother Wound. The questions are: How deep is the wound? How long is it? Has it been repaired?)

Over the years of working with men and women as their psychotherapist, teacher, or coach, I've witnessed shared experiences of self-doubt, self-criticism, and emotional pain stemming from a Mother Wound. If you have these experiences, there is nothing wrong with you—no, not at all! I would ask: What happened to you? What did you experience? What is true for you right now?

Regardless of your gender or sexual identity, you may have incurred a Mother Wound and suffer from its effects. And you can learn to overcome it.

Healing

Mother Wounds are not a negative life sentence but rather a path to growth. The wound's length, width, and depth will decide the type of healing journey being called forth. You are taking an exciting step toward healing the Mother Wound you've been carrying for much too long. Be aware that Overcoming a Mother Wound (OCMW) is not a one-and-done or a quick fix. Overcoming a Mother Wound takes time, support, and developing a new perspective.

This book is meant to create an educational and healing experience for you. It can teach you how to connect with yourself in new ways, learn mind/body concepts that can guide you in understanding yourself better, let go of old relational patterns from your personal history and experiences, and create new, yet-to-be-discovered gems inside of yourself that will help you navigate your next best steps.

We focus on the effects on adults who have had a difficult relationship with their maternal figure and how to clean, clear, and move beyond their wounds. All sexual identities may have a mother wound, and sharing these similarities and differences promotes healing globally.

We start with the foundations in order to be supportive. We review your unique relationship with your mother and possible attachment styles using art and writing prompts. (I use "mother" to represent your early caretaker(s), whoever they may have been.)

Then, we consider your attachment style in relation to your Mother Wound.

We will then engage in a variety of exercises and processes to clarify the ways in which your wound arises in your mind and experiences and learn techniques to release them, allowing you to see yourself and your relationships with others in a new light.

If you use the workbook as a guide, follow the prompts, exercises, and suggested resources, or join one of my groups (information about my course and groups can be found in the Appendix), you will build a stronger internal voice that you will slowly but surely learn to trust, honor, and appreciate.

This Workbook

This workbook is structured as a learning experience for those seeking to understand better how they have been affected by early childhood experiences. The knowledge here is to help you learn, grow, and experience support in ways you may not have imagined before.

This book can be a stand-alone guide for self-discovery and healing, or it can accompany the online course that includes group coaching calls for those wanting more support.

My approach is gentle and supportive. We start off slowly, letting you orient yourself to the material and get acquainted with the exercises. The exercises and prompts are simple but by no means easy. We are not running a sprint here. We need to take our time; your wound did not develop overnight and is not healed overnight either. I suggest completing a chapter a week, including exercises, and being as consistent as possible.

Each chapter includes an introduction to the content of the chapter's theme and exercises that will support learning and absorbing the material, as well as a conclusion summing up the main points that were covered.

You will be instructed with prompts for art making and writing to practice the concepts in real-time. The exercises expand your experience to a level that is beyond "knowing" the material. We want not just your head involved but also your body, emotions, and sensations. This is what I refer to as a "bottom-up" versus a "top-down" perspective. You may have some "top-down" shifts and lights switched on in your mind as you read, and that is great. But we need "bottom-up," felt experiences for real change to take place.

With bottom-up techniques, the information is not just an idea in your head but a felt experience in your body. Healing requires that we involve the whole body, including the nervous system, which in turn includes our heart rate, breath, ability to be present, and ability to recognize our level of distress or calm. At times, you may want to rush through an exercise or take a break. Please notice that urge; it is natural. You may slow down, but please try not to abandon the exercise. If you do the work, you will experience a shift. My hope is that you take the time to honor your process.

For the writing exercises, lined pages are included inside the chapters and at the end of the book, so you have a place where you can practice the exercises, respond to the prompts, and add your thoughts and feelings, your expectations, your accomplishments, your disappointments, or random musings. We recommend you have an additional journal or art pad dedicated to your **OCMW (Overcoming the Mother Wound)** experience so you are not limited by the size of the book's pages, and you are able to say whatever you want to say for as long as you need to say it.

We will also engage in artmaking **(see Appendix A for suggested art supplies for the book)**.

It's been found that artmaking increases neural functioning by activating crucial parts of the brain. For instance, the hypothalamus, a tiny area that can release hormones and regulate the body, as well as the orbitofrontal cortex associated with impulse control and decision-making, are stimulated while making art. This activation improves brain function and has been shown to have an impact on brain wave patterns, the nervous system, and our emotions. As it does this, it also calms the amygdala, where we hold emotional memories (our alarm center). Making art, your brain gets a chance to recharge, and your body gets to relax. Art can be a catalyst for well-being and creating balance in your life.

Artmaking is a beautiful, raw, genuine human experience. It is also a deceptively powerful tool.

If we have been wounded in any way, those wounds may surface while making art. Feeling these wounds arise is completely natural. If you feel or think something while making art, pause on meaning-making and listen. This is precious information wanting attention, that's all. If you notice a desire to stop, shut down, or destroy what you have made, pause. Put your art aside, and come back to it a day, a week, or a month later. Has your response to your art changed?

To initiate you into your healing journey, I'd like you to now do two preliminary exercises: one written exercise, and one artistic exercise. These exercises (assessments) will measure where you are now and where you will be at the end of the Overcoming the Mother Wound book.

We start with a Mother Wound Self-Assessment and a Mother-Child Art Prompt, and at the end of the book, you will repeat these assessments to gauge your progress. These are tools to help you track your progress, see how this book has helped you, and assess whether there is more work to be done.

Assessment #1

Mother Wound Self-Assessment: *APPENDIX I*

Below are questions written in the first person. Please answer to the best of your ability:

1. When I wake up in the morning,
    1. It is the best time of the day; let me stretch, move, and look around; I'm glad to wake up.
    2. I think about all the stuff I have to do and can't stay in bed, so I get up.
    3. I'm annoyed that I have to get up, but I just want to stay in bed and not be bothered.
2. When I go to bed at night,
    1. I fall asleep easily and usually sleep straight till it's time to get up.
    2. I toss and turn, thinking about the day and wondering about tomorrow.
    3. It doesn't matter if I fall asleep early or late; I wake up through the night and often have disturbing dreams.
3. When I look at myself in the mirror,
    1. I see a beautiful soul that has done a great job with their life so far.
    2. I see someone that needs to do a lot of work but might be okay someday.
    3. I see someone that needs help, and I wish I knew how to help myself better.
4. My friendships
    1. I have a few close friends, especially 1 or 2, who I confide in deeply.
    2. I like people, but I keep meeting demanding and critical people.
    3. It is hard for me to get close to other people; I don't think they like me.
5. My romantic relations
    1. I am in a long-term serious relationship where I feel accepted and supported.

2. I am in an "on again-off again" passionate relationship, which is my usual pattern.

3. I usually get involved with someone who is not available or is abusive.

6. When I have time to myself

    1. I like to take time to recharge with a creative endeavor or spend time in nature.

    2. I like to be busy; retail therapy usually does the trick.

    3. I zone out and get lost, unsure of what to do. Then I start to berate myself for not using my time better.

7. When I meet someone new,

    1. I am curious to find out who they are and for them to know who I am.

    2. I prefer to let them reach out if they want to get to know me.

    3. New people make me nervous; I don't think they'll like me anyway.

8. If I need to make an important decision,

    1. I sit quietly, view the situation, and ask for inner guidance.

    2. I write down all the pros and cons methodically and see what makes sense.

    3. I ask other people what I should do after exhausting the above options.

Tally your results to keep for the end of the workbook. Add how many you put for each: As, Bs, and Cs. You can put these results in a sealed envelope and keep it in a safe place for a later date.

Remember, there are no right or wrong answers; this is a judgment-free zone. We simply want to understand your current relationship with yourself and then assess your relationship to your *Self* after you have completed the exercises in this book.

Assessment #2

Mother-Child Drawing Prompt: *APPENDIX H*

Gather art materials of your choice, which may or may not be from the list provided in Appendix A.

Find a comfortable place where you will not be disturbed for 10 to 20 minutes.

Settle in your space, take a deep breath in, hold it for a moment, and then let it slowly as if you are blowing through a straw.

I suggest doing that at least one more time to activate your rest and digest or parasympathetic nervous system.

Then, think of a time in your past, go back as far as you'd like, and see what image comes up of you and your mother.

Draw this picture of you and your mother.

Add the date and title of the drawing.

Set the drawing aside for now.

Lastly, before moving into the first chapter, I recommend choosing a book from the suggested reading list in Appendix B and using it as an ancillary support for this workbook experience.

And note: this book can be read on its own or used as a compendium to go with the Overcoming the Mother Wound Course, a self-study course with a membership site for community, accountability, and support.

CHAPTER 1:
SETTLING

Overcoming the
Mother Wound

A: SETTLING

Before we go on a journey, we usually prepare. This could be packing, planning, or gearing up, so to speak. That is how I look at settling the nervous system so we are able to fully engage and enjoy what we are learning.

In this section, you will learn a settling and an intention-setting exercise to prepare you for what is ahead.

SETTLING EXERCISE *APPENDIX L*

Find a comfortable place where you won't be disturbed.

Sit comfortably. Feel your feet meeting the ground and sense any support to your body. Is the support beneath you? Behind you?

Start noticing your breath. See if you can count how long you inhale and how long you exhale.

Sometimes just noticing your breath is settling.

Some people find it helpful to breathe in for the count of 4, pause for the count of 4, exhale to the count of 4, and pause to the count of 4 before repeating that for 4 more rounds. It is also called the "square breath."

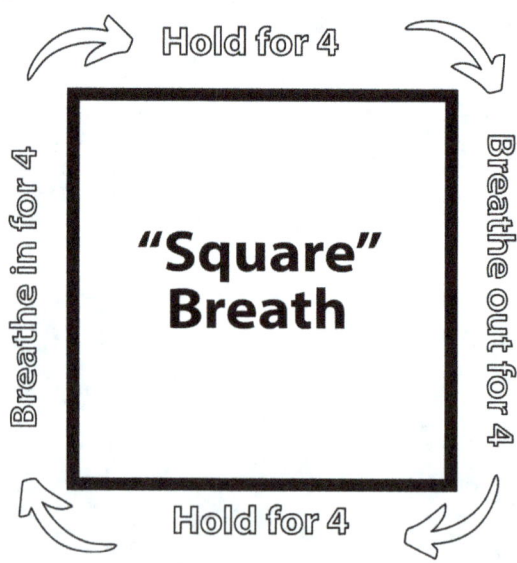

When you feel settled, that is a great time to set an intention.

SET AN INTENTION EXERCISE *APPENDIX M*

Stand and feel your feet on the ground.

Bounce a little up and down to feel the weight of your body.

As you breathe, feel your breath all the way into your belly and then exhale fully.

Count how long you inhale, then double that as you exhale.

Do that about three times. If this makes you dizzy, perhaps breathe for fewer counts.

Breathing in for a count of three and out for six is usually a comfortable count.

Take a moment to get a feel for what it is you need today.

<u>**You can ask yourself:**</u>

What would I like to take in from today's lesson?

What would I like to bring to today's lesson?

Let an **intention** for today come to mind. Accept whatever comes.

Now, stand with your legs a little further than your shoulders in a "horse stance" (as if riding a horse and your feet are in stirrups). Point your feet straight forward with your feet flat on the ground.

Bounce, bend your knees gently, and feel the ground beneath you.

Start with **hands on top of the heart**, the left hand on top of the right for women, the right hand on top of left for men (a qigong tradition, but you can do whatever is comfortable), hold there for a moment and set an intention for your today.

Inhale and expand that intention as you **reach your arms out**, opening your heart space, stretching your arms wide, and opening your intention to the world.

Exhale, pull in (**hug in**), and receive what you need to support this intention; wrap yourself in an embrace.

Repeat this for a total of three times.

B: SELF-REFLECTION; WHAT WE THINK EXERCISE

The exercises below start with writing. You may use the pages in this workbook or have a separate journal dedicated to the OCMW process.

Please answer these journal prompts **and save them for later exercises** in this book:

1. What are my hopes, dreams, and wishes once I discover the contents of this book?

_____
_____
_____
_____
_____
_____
_____

2. How do I ask for help?

3. How do I feel when I ask for help?

4. Think of important characteristics you love in yourself or someone else; write at least five in your journal or below. A **positive characteristic** can be love, support, kindness, or ANYTHING in between. What works for YOU is what matters. Right or wrong does not belong. Remember: if you want to borrow something you value in another, that works too.

1.
2.
3.
4.
5.

TIP: Keep these **positive comments** from question number four handy for future meditations.

C: ART TIME

YOUR TREE OF STRENGTH

This is your first "Art Time." This book includes a lot of art making. Art making, if fun, relieves and releases stress.

It has been scientifically found to reduce cortisol levels, a stress hormone that can weaken our immune system if left unchecked.

We use art in this book to increase our sense of well-being and deepen our experience. Did you know that when Neurons (from the brain) "fire" together, they "wire" together?

When you think about something and have a positive experience while doing it, you build positive connections in your gray matter, which means you support neural plasticity (growth and change in the brain).

Cool, huh?

The Tree of Strength is a great support for building on neuroplasticity. This exercise helps remind us of things about ourselves we either forgot, did not realize, or valued.

Directions are below; an example is on the next page for your reference.

Grab your 11" x 17" paper, pencils, pens, and markers.

Lay one hand on the paper, and your fingers spread with part of your arm on the paper.

Trace your arm and hand, leaving the tips of the **finger's tips open.**

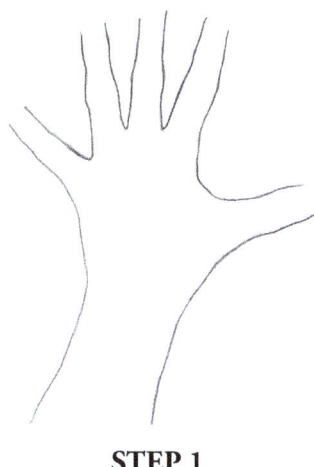

STEP 1

Lift arm.

At the end of the open fingertips, extend the drawing to create more branches.

Draw several leaves at the end of the "branches," making them large enough to **write in each one.**

On each leaf, write one thing that helps you get through a difficult time – personal strengths, coping strategies, enjoyable activities, supportive people, etc.

Create as many leaves as you want, but no less than 5.

STEP 2

When finished:

Look at your Tree of Strength; be with it for a few moments.

Use the space below, or take out your journal and explore with these prompts:

Before I started this exercise, I thought it was _____. When I finished, I realized it was _____.

I found out that my supporters are mostly _____.

I was surprised that

What I most like about my supports are:

The hardest part of this exercise is:

The best part of this exercise is:

Believing I have support makes me:

TIP: Keep track of your experiences in this book or in your journal. It will help support you in your work of Overcoming the Mother Wound, and you may be surprised to see your progress when you look through it at the end.

You can repeat this and the other lessons as often as possible. Take it at your own pace, although I suggest weekly if you can.

D: SUPPORT WORK

Each Chapter has "Support Work" to support your learning and deepening of your experiences. These sections are meant to be enjoyable and fun, allowing you time to be creative. They are an integral part of the effectiveness of this workbook.

Gather your art materials: *APPENDIX A*

Art Materials List

11x17" paper

12x 12 multi-color paper

Blank paper large enough for a dinner size plate

Colored Crayons

Colored Pencils

Compass or dinner size plate for circle

Cray-pas

Glue Sticks

Journal for Writing

Markers

Paintbrush (s)

Pen (s)

Sketching Pencil

Sharpie or black marker

Stones (rocks)

Water-based paints

Your favorite drawing materials

Create Circles:

Start drawing circles on a piece of paper. Use your compass or a dinner-size plate to draw a circle on paper that is at least 12" x 12." We need at least one for lesson 2. We will use them often, so you might want to make a couple of extras.

E: CONCLUSION

In this Chapter, we learned how to **settle** when we may be feeling a lot of emotions at once and a grounded, embodied way to **set an intention** for the day.

You created your first piece of art as a supportive resource, your **Tree of Strength**, to help remind you of things that help you get through a difficult time.

We included extra Support Work that will help set you up for future exercises using the circle.

I will explain more about working with the circle and why I have included them in this book.

CHAPTER 2:
ATTACHMENT STYLES

Overcoming the
Mother Wound

A: ATTACHMENT STYLES - Child

Let's talk about the big "A" Attachment.

We need to talk about it, especially in a book with a focus on our primary attachment figure.

Attachment Overview

Awareness of our attachment style is a vital step in the healing process. This key insight serves as a tool for reflecting on our lived experiences and understanding them more deeply to move forward.

As human beings, we cannot survive without a sense of attachment. Like a young cub in the wild, as children, we must be held, fed, and kept warm. Although we come into this world whole, we are helpless and defenseless when we come out of the womb. Attachment styles are formed in this early stage of life in direct response to the ways our earliest caregivers treat us.

As our primary attachment figure, the mother plays a significant role in attachment style development. How we are nurtured, seen, and loved by our mother shapes our inner world. No matter how seemingly small or insignificant, the mother's demeanor, words, and actions communicate messages about our worth, safety, and place in the world. As young and impressionable sponges, we soak up these messages as they slowly become our truth.

The early mother/child dynamic has deep and lasting effects on how we function in adulthood.

Seemingly every aspect of our being is impacted - from our personality traits to our relationship habits. How we experience our mother in childhood drives the development of our internalized voices, shapes how we interact in interpersonal relationships, and helps or hinders our ability to trust others.

Pause and take a moment to breathe. Beginning to unpack your attachment to your mother is hard work.

I hope you feel comforted in knowing that you are far from alone in unpacking this complex topic. Professionals and researchers have devoted their careers to understanding attachment styles for decades.

Below is a helpful graphic and findings from child development researchers (John Bowlby and Mary Ainsworth) that illustrate and explain the various types of attachment styles:

Secure: Your needs were met pretty consistently. Your thoughts and feelings were acknowledged, your personal space was valued and respected, and you knew someone was there if you needed them.

Ambivalent/Anxious: Your needs were sometimes neglected and sometimes acknowledged. They were never met in a consistent and dependable way. This may be physical, sexual, and/or emotional.

Avoidant: You experienced neglect or abuse and were maybe even punished for relying on a caretaker. Again, this may have been physical, sexual, and/or emotional.

Disorganized: This happens when there is a lack of clear boundaries. Who is the child, and who is the parent? This style stems from inconsistent parenting - the same parent becomes a source of comfort and fear.

PROMPT:

Is there an Attachment Style that resonates more deeply than the rest? If so, which?

_____
_____
_____

You may be one type, or most likely a combination, depending on where you are, who you are with, what you are doing, and how you are being received.

B: ATTACHMENT STYLES

ADULT

Let's look at **Adult Attachment** Styles (developed by John Bowlby and Mary Ainsworth).

The attachment styles look very different from when we were little:

Below are attachment styles affecting adult women and men; as you can see, these styles are the same, but the individual responses differ, depending on multiple factors. I have included vignettes for each style, for male and female genders. See if you resonate with any of these. (My apologies if I have not included your gender identity; I would love to hear from you on how to represent your experience).

WOMEN

SECURE:

Comfortable expressing emotions openly.

They are able to depend on their loved ones and, in return, let others rely on them, too.

Relationships are based on honesty, tolerance, and emotional closeness.

Childhood Experience: Although no caregiver can always be perfect, your needs were consistently met. Your thoughts and feelings were acknowledged, your personal space was valued and respected, and you knew someone was there if you needed them.

Adult Experience: You generally feel content in your life, work, and relationships. You are self-aware and comfortable feeling and expressing your emotions. Your social experience is easy and warm, and you're able to build meaningful relationships, both romantic and platonic.

Mother Experience: Molly comes from a stable enough home where her thoughts and feelings matter. When she came out as a lesbian at 15 years old, her family embraced her for having the courage to be honest, and her mother let her know she can come to her with any other feelings she may be having.

Now: Molly loves her job, her girlfriend, and her home. When her downstairs neighbors leave smelly garbage on the stoop below her window, she goes and asks them to put the garbage inside the can. While it may be uncomfortable, she's able to express her needs and set boundaries.

AMBIVALENT/ANXIOUS:

Possesses a strong fear of abandonment.

Rely on others for approval, support, and reassurance that they are loved.

Tend to have a negative self-image while having a positive view of others.

Childhood Experience: Your needs weren't met in a reliable or dependable way. Whether physically or emotionally, you weren't completely seen and nurtured. When you felt big feelings, you were often dismissed rather than receiving comfort and reassurance.

Adult Experience: You often feel paralyzed by a deep fear of abandonment and rejection. Low self-esteem and negative self-talk take up much of your mental real estate. Interpersonal relationships are challenging, and you often display a tendency towards clinginess.

Mother Experience: Jodi was a joyful, creative child who loved to dance and sing. When Jodi was invited to a final performance in elementary school, her mother refused to take her because she was too scared to drive at night. Jodi began to cry, and her mother told her the performance was not a big deal and to go to her room if she wanted to cry.

Now: Jane has a full-time job and makes enough money to pay the bills. She wants more romance in her life and keeps finding partners who are attracted to her, but they don't stick around. Her last boyfriend, Matt, ghosted her after 2 months of dating and her 20 texts.

AVOIDANT:

Tend to have a positive view of themselves.

Don't want to depend on others, have others depend on them, or seek support.

Avoid emotional closeness and often hide or suppress their feelings.

Childhood Experience: You experienced neglect or abuse from your caregiver(s). You were often punished, shamed, or dismissed when you looked for care and support. The neglect or abuse may have been physical, sexual, or emotional.

Adult Experience: You come across as confident and self-sufficient on the outside. You experience your sense of worth from your achievements and success in life. You find it hard to let in emotional or physical intimacy and, as a result, struggle to build healthy relationships.

Mother Experience: Rebecca comes from a household where feelings had no place unless mom or dad were raging about their relationship. Mom took center stage, and Dad slipped away and eventually left. Through this, Rebecca was born with buck teeth and a speech impediment. She was teased relentlessly by her family for how she ate and what she sounded like. Her mother would look away as her brother and father would laugh at their own insults.

Now: Rebecca is competent, confident, and good at whatever she does. She is absorbed by work and has occasional one-night stands. She is not interested in romantic relationships because they're too time-consuming and take her off her "game."

DISORGANIZED:

Struggle with emotional regulation.

Desire intimacy and closeness but struggle to trust and depend on them.

Avoid strong emotional attachment due to a fear of being hurt and disappointed.

Childhood Experience: You experienced a blurring of boundaries and a lack of clarity on your role as a child. The ways your caregiver(s) parented were inconsistent. While being a source of comfort, your parent was also a source of fear.

Adult Experience: Trusting others does not come naturally or easily. You're inconsistent in the ways you connect with others and build relationships. You might suffer from mental health challenges like substance abuse, anxiety, or depression.

Mother Experience: Gilda's mother was unhappy and hoped the birth of a daughter would change that. Mom found Gilda demanding and ungrateful as an infant. When Gilda began to walk and talk, Mom would find Gilda more amusing and would love to dress her up and parade her with her on errands. When Gilda would get tired or hungry, she would get spanked for being selfish. Gilda found comfort in school. At 42, she is still studying to change her career again.

Now: Gilda shows up in one of my groups. She either wants to comment on whoever or whatever the topic is or becomes withdrawn and silent during the group. When she does comment, it is to give her opinion rather than to share her feelings.

Did you find yourself identifying with one of these styles? Or you identified parts of each of the attachment styles. Either way, we will be exploring these more so that we can properly understand your relationship with your mother or mother figure and start the healing process.

MEN

Comfortable expressing emotions openly.

They are able to depend on their loved ones and, in return, let others rely on them, too.

Relationships are based on honesty, tolerance, and emotional closeness.

SECURE

Childhood Experience: Although no caregiver can always be perfect, your needs were consistently met. Your thoughts and feelings were acknowledged, your personal space was valued and respected, and you knew someone was there if you needed them.

Adult Experience: You generally feel content in your life, work, and relationships. You are self-aware and comfortable feeling and expressing your emotions. Your social experience is easy and warm, and you're able to build meaningful relationships, both romantic and platonic.

Mother Experience: Michael comes from a stable enough home where his feelings, preferences, and insights are acknowledged and valued. When he came out as gay at 14 years old, he was supported by his family and embraced for his honesty. Michael's mother let him know he can come to her with any other feelings he may be having, and his father accepted him no differently than before and let him know he is still Michael and loves him dearly.

Now: Michael loves his job in a startup, is engaged to his boyfriend, and takes pride in his manicure. When his boyfriend needs to leave town for a 2-week business trip, he feels left and lonely. Michael wants to support his fiancée's career but struggles. While it may be uncomfortable, Michael lets his partner know his feelings, and they both work out how and when they will connect during those 2 weeks. Michael trusts his partner and can express his needs and set boundaries.

AMBIVALENT/ANXIOUS:

Possesses a strong fear of abandonment.

Rely on others for approval, support, and reassurance that they are loved.

Tend to have a negative self-image while having a positive view of others.

Childhood Experience: Your needs weren't met in a reliable or dependable way. Whether physically or emotionally, you weren't completely seen and nurtured. When you felt big feelings, you were often dismissed rather than receiving comfort and reassurance.

Adult Experience: You often feel paralyzed by a deep fear of abandonment and rejection. Low self-esteem and negative self-talk take up much of your mental real estate. Interpersonal relationships are challenging, and you often display a tendency towards clinginess.

Mother Experience: Jim was a playful, creative child who loved to dance and sing. When Jim was invited to perform for his school play in elementary school, his mother refused to take him because she was more concerned about what her husband and the PTA would say. Jim began to cry, and his mother told him the performance was not important, that he was embarrassing himself, and to wipe his tears before anyone else saw them.

Now: Jim works as a full-time clerk and makes just enough money to pay his bills. Jim wants spark and romance in his life but keeps finding partners who think his ideas are frivolous and immature. Jim would agree and laugh it off. In relationships, Jim would do whatever his date wanted to do to keep the relationship from ending. His last lover borrowed 1K and then skipped town - until Jim spotted her at a music festival 3 years later and did not bring it up when they spoke.

AVOIDANT:

Tend to have a positive view of themselves.

Don't want to depend on others, have others depend on them, or seek support.

Avoid emotional closeness and often hide or suppress their feelings.

Childhood Experience: You experienced neglect or abuse from your caregiver(s). When you looked for care and support, you were often punished, shamed, or dismissed. The neglect or abuse may have been physical, sexual, or emotional.

Adult Experience: On the outside, you come across as confident and self-sufficient. You experience your sense of worth from your achievements and success in life. You find it hard to let in emotional or physical intimacy and, as a result, struggle to build healthy relationships.

Mother Experience: Robert comes from a household where feelings had no place unless his parents were raging about money and his father's infidelity. Mom took center stage and was the ultimate victim; Dad slipped away and eventually left. Robert was born with strong features and would later grow into a handsome man. As a child, his family teased him relentlessly about his big eyes, ears, and nose and likened him to a jungle animal. His mother would walk out of the room when the teasing began, leaving him with his older brother, sister, and father.

Now: Robert is super competent and a highly sought-after lawyer. He is absorbed by work and going to the gym. Relationally he will have occasional one-night stands, but romance is not a priority. It's too time-consuming, and he believes makes him lose focus.

DISORGANIZED:

Struggle with emotional regulation.

Desire intimacy and closeness but struggle to trust and depend on them.

Avoid strong emotional attachment due to a fear of being hurt and disappointed.

Childhood Experience: You experienced a blurring of boundaries and a lack of clarity on your role as a child. The ways your caregiver(s) parented were inconsistent. While being a source of comfort, your parent was also a source of fear.

Adult Experience: Trusting others does not come naturally or easily. You're inconsistent in the ways you connect with others and build relationships. You might suffer from mental health challenges like substance abuse, anxiety, or depression.

Mother Experience: Greg's mother was unhappy and hoped the birth of a daughter would change that, but her child was a boy. Mom blamed Greg for not being a girl and saw him as a tricky infant. When Greg began to walk and talk, Mom would find him more amusing, dress him in girls' clothes, and take him with her on errands. When Greg no longer wanted to wear girls' clothes, he would get spanked for being selfish. Greg found comfort in school, where he could wear boys' clothes without punishment.

Now: Greg is a shy, angry client. He found work in the textile industry and wished he had a wider circle of friends. He is suspicious of my interest in him and wonders how therapy can help with his difficulty trusting others.

Jot down your thoughts, memories, and insights on your attachment style(s) here:

PROMPTS:

Did you identify with one of these styles? If so, which?

Do you remember a story that goes with that?

If you identified with more than one, which were they?

We will be exploring these more to better understand your relationship with your mother or mother figure and start the healing process.

B: SUPPORTWORK

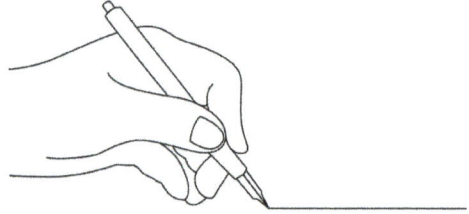

Use these writing prompts in your journal or below to explore your experience of your attachment style(s) and how it connects to the mother wound.

1. Which Attachment Style resonates with your experience the most? Which resonates the least?

   _____
   _____
   _____
   _____
   _____

2. Which Attachment Styles did you experience from your caregivers in childhood?

   _____
   _____
   _____
   _____

3. When I feel a strong negative emotion towards somebody I like, it is easiest for me to:

   a. Pretend it's not there and keep the conversation light.

   b Bring it up and hope we can work through this

   c Blame the other person for making me feel that way

   d Annoyed, but note it and think to myself to bring it up if it happens again.

C: QUIZ

You may have a better sense of your attachment style now.

What about understanding attachment styles as a whole?

Try this Quiz, and check your answers in the Key below:

1. I am more worried about what others will think of my answers rather than what I think about my answers I am acting from a(n) _____ attachment style.

2. I can't finish my lesson on time and decide it is stupid anyway, so why bother? I am acting from a(n) _____ attachment style.

3. When I say to myself:

    a. "If I post things my friends don't like on Facebook, I will be unfriended." I am acting from a(n) _____ attachment style.

    b. "When people give me compliments, it's because they want something from me." I am acting from a(n) _____ attachment style.

    c. "If I say what I mean, other people will judge me." I am acting from a(n) _____ attachment style.

    d. "This may be helpful for you, but I don't need this." I am acting from a(n) _____ attachment style.

    e. "This makes me feel vulnerable and uncomfortable. I need to stop and take a break to comfort myself for a few minutes. I am acting from a(n) _____ attachment style.

    f. "I don't trust this group; they are pretending to be nice. That only means something bad is going to happen." I am acting from a(n) _____ attachment style.

KEY

1. Anxious/Ambivalent

2. Avoidant

3. a. Anxious/Ambivalent

    b. Avoidant

    c. Anxious/Ambivalent

    d. Avoidant

    e. Secure

    f. Disorganized

D: CONCLUSION

This module included an overview of Attachment Styles, formed by the well-known child development researchers John Bowlby and Mary Ainsworth.

We also learned that as infants, we depend on having our needs met, and how they are met defines our attachment style. We can either be one specific style or a variation depending on our situation. These attachment styles carry through into adulthood and can affect how we are in our relationships.

We looked at the spectrum from infancy to adulthood, for men and for women.

Case vignettes were shared (identities and other details changed to protect their identity), to illustrate the material more fully.

You may want to refer to this Module when we dive into the types of Mother Wounds and how they came to be.

CHAPTER 3:
RESOURCING

Overcoming the
Mother Wound

A: WHAT YOU NEED

In this chapter, we will start by settling our nervous system, learning about Resources, and then creating art, TWICE, to explore what we need and are ready to let go of. Art and writing prompts will be below, so have your materials handy.

FOR THIS LESSON, YOU WILL NEED:

- About an hour to an hour and a half, but you can break it into more than one sitting.
- The circle you created in Chapter One's support work. If you have not yet drawn a circle or two, you can take a dinner plate or a drawing compass and draw a big circle in the middle of a large blank piece of paper.
- Your journal.
- Your "positive words" list from Chapter One's self-reflection exercise.
- Your Tree of Strength
- Rocks, paints, brushes, coloring materials.

Start with the Settling and Intention Setting Exercises. See below.

SETTLING EXERCISE: *APPENDIX L*

Find a comfortable place where you won't be disturbed.

Sit comfortably. Feel your feet meeting the ground and sense any support to your body. Is the support beneath you? Behind you?

Start noticing your breath. See if you can count how long you inhale and how long you exhale.

Sometimes just noticing your breath is settling.

Some people find it helpful to breathe in for the count of 4, pause for the count of 4, exhale to the count of 4, and pause to the count of 4 before repeating that for 4 more rounds. It is also called the "square breath."

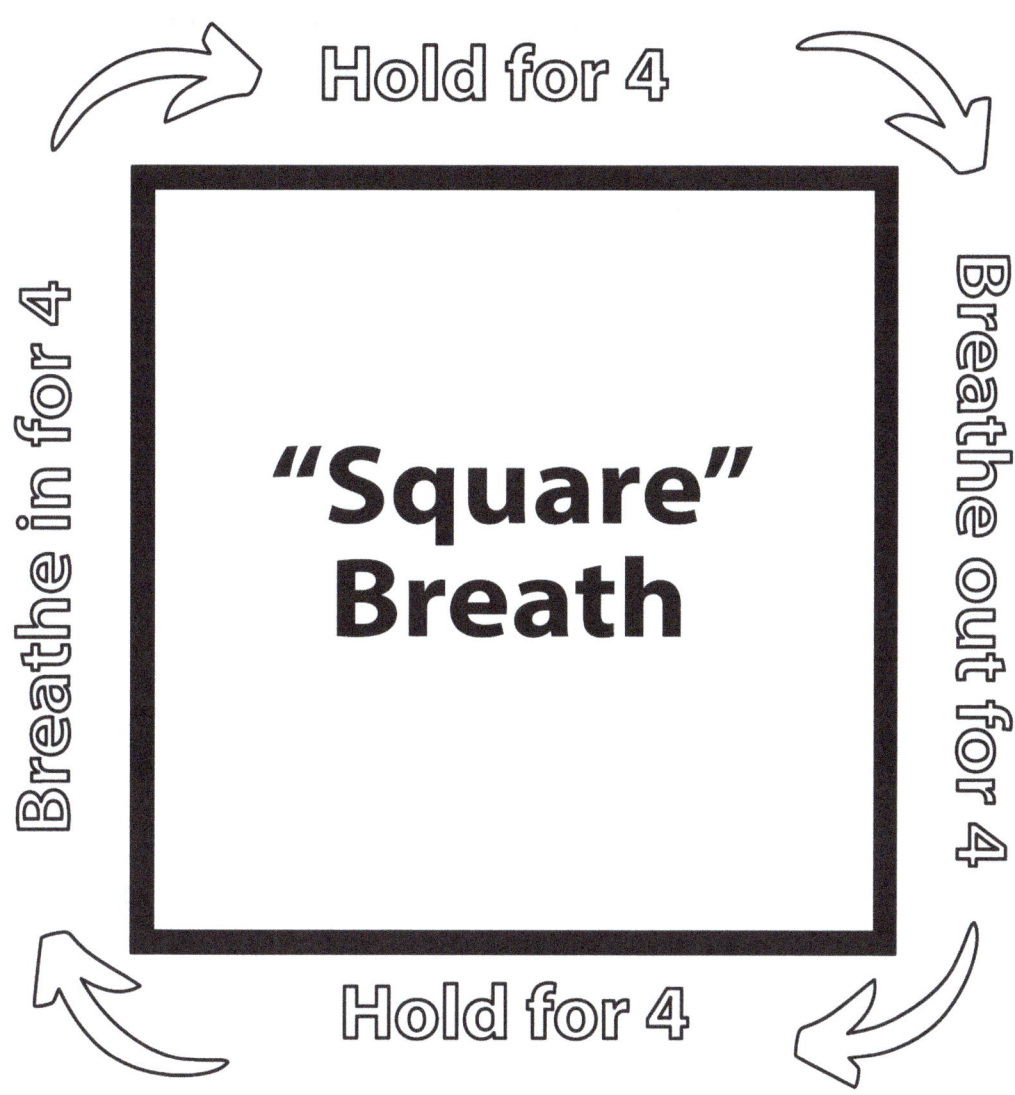

When you feel settled, that is a great time to set an intention.

SET AN INTENTION EXERCISE *APPENDIX M*:

Stand and feel your feet on the ground.

Bounce a little up and down to feel the weight of your body. As you breathe, feel your breath all the way into your belly and exhale fully.

Perhaps counting how long you inhale and then doubling that count as you exhale. Do that about 3 times. If this makes you dizzy, perhaps breathe for fewer counts. 3 in and 6 out is usually a comfortable count.

Take a moment to feel in for what it is you need today.

What would you like to take in from today's lesson?

What would you like to bring to today's lesson?

Let an Intention for today come to mind.

Accept whatever comes.

Now, stand with your legs a little further than your shoulders, in a "horse stance" as if riding a horse as if your feet are in stirrups.

Point your feet straight forward with your feet flat on the ground.

Bounce, bend your knees gently and feel the ground beneath your feet.

Start with hands on top of the heart, the left hand on top of the right for women, the right hand on top of the left for men (a qigong tradition but you can do whatever is comfortable), hold there for a moment, and set an intention for your lesson.

Inhale and expand that intention out as you reach your arms out, opening your heart space, stretching your arms wide, and opening your intention to the world.

Exhale, pull in, and receive what you need (hug in) to support this intention; wrap yourself in an embrace.

Repeat this a total of 3 times.

Open your intention from your heart and hug in and receive what you need.

Okay, ready to move forward?

B: ABOUT RESOURCING

We've talked about settling and how to ground ourselves and connect with our nervous system, and now I'd like to share a little about resourcing.

A resource can be in the form of a person, an object, an experience, or a feeling. In this course, I'm referring to a resource as something that is intended to provide physical, emotional, and spiritual support to you as you navigate your thoughts and feelings.

Resourcing is a way to strengthen external and/or internal connections to feelings of support that already exist and may be hidden or may have been forgotten.

Resources, in particular internal resources, help by being comforting and grounding when we need extra support or are working with uncomfortable feelings.

Below are simple but effective exercises that are external resources but create an internal sense of calm while you are in the creative process and afterward.

See for yourself!

Before we go any further, let's check in:

Look around your space and notice what you are drawn to.

How does it make you feel?

See if you can find something that makes you feel closest to your Best Self, the part of you that appreciates the beauty inside and outside of you. Whatever that is today. Is it a color? A smell? Is it moving? Is it still?

Notice the qualities of what you are drawn to that help you feel settled and ready for this exercise.

Have your paper with a circle on it. Today we will use the circle to help you with your intention.

A circle is the shape of the Earth, the moon, and the sun. The circle is a symbol of wholeness and completion. For some, the circle has spiritual and religious significance. For others, it can have mathematical significance.

The circle is also the shape of a Mandala, which is the Sanskrit word for circle. Mandalas are a symbol of the Universe and are meant to help transform ordinary minds into enlightened ones. Helping to focus attention on the self, quieting the mind, and promoting healing.

C: MANDALA EXERCISE
- WHAT YOU NEED - RESOURCE -

ART TIME

INSTRUCTIONS:

Gather your materials, and choose from my suggestions:

Paper with Circle

Pencils, Pens, Crayons, Markers, Paints

Glue, Magazines

Found objects.

Have your paper with a circle on it near or in front of you, as well as writing or coloring materials of your choice, photographs, or magazine images work too. Take as long or short of time as you need. Usually, between 10 and 30 minutes is enough time for this exercise.

CREATE YOUR CIRCLE

Inside the circle:

Inside your circle, you will put what **you need today.** You can do this with colors, lines, drawn or cut-out images –whatever best expresses what you need today.

Outside the circle:

Put what you want to **let go of** today outside the circle.

Reinforce the thickness of that circle if there are any intrusions. Deepen or thicken the circle line to help separate what you need and want to let go of today. Make that line as thick as you want!

Sample of What You Need Mandala

SUPPORTIVE PROMPTS

Use your own Journal or the space below to answer these prompts. They are here to help you delve deeper into this Art-Making Experience:

What is it like to ask for what you want?

What is it like to put what you don't want outside of your circle?

Did you have an overlap? What you want is also what you don't want but has a different name.

Were you able to create a boundary between what you need now and what you don't want?

Remember, this is a judgment-free zone. You are exploring here, and there is no right or wrong.

D: GUIDED MEDITATION: BEST SELF RESOURCE

Below is a meditation to support you.

Recommendation: record the words below and then play the audio when you are in a place where you can close your eyes and listen.

When you see the word "pause," do not say the word out loud but be still and "pause" in silence.

Or have someone you love record it for you. Whichever way best suits you today.

Give yourself 10 – 30 minutes to settle, listen, and respond in writing or art-making about what you see, feel, or whatever else you experienced.

BEST SELF *APPENDIX D*

Start by making yourself comfortable, lying down or sitting.

Begin to notice your breath, inhaling to the count of 3 and exhaling to the count of 6; continue inhaling and exhaling, spending a little more time on the exhalation.

Soften or close your eyes as you listen to these words:

Think of a time, a moment, when you felt like your true self, *pause.*

However far back or far you need to go, see what comes to you, *pause.*

What was that like?

Is it something you experienced?

Something you completed, accomplished and felt good about.

Did you dream about it?

Take a moment and scan over your life; what pops up?

How did it make you feel?

Whether anyone noticed or not, you knew how good you felt. Feel that feeling, *pause.*

Notice how your body feels, *pause.*

What do your eyes see? *pause.*

How do you stand? pause, what is your energy like?

This is your BEST SELF. Take a moment and look at your best self.

What do you see? Stand next to your Best Self. How does it feel to be with your Best Self?

Take a moment and take in what it is like to be with your best self.

Remember these important feelings and characteristics.

After listening, here are some questions you could ask yourself and explore in your journal:

My best self feels like _____.

My best self looks like _____.

I'd like to say to my best self _____.

My best self tells me _____.

I'd like to share that _____.

Create a drawing here or in your journal as a great way to have your best self in physical representation, to bring forward with you as you continue along in this book, and as a reference whenever you may want or need to remember your Best Self.

I'll refer back to "Your Best Self" and allow you to connect to Your Best Self in future exercises.

E: SUPPORT STONES - RESOURCE

ART TIME

A simple and powerful resource to have at the ready is Support Stones, or Rocks.

All you will need are rocks (washed and dried), paints, and brushes. If you don't have any rocks handy, you can use any object, preferably from nature, that you can paint.

Support Stones are a great way to embody your resources. You can create some now and more at any time the Resource Spirit moves you. For example, as you discover a new "resource" or something or someone that feels supportive, paint a rock that goes with that resource and then add words to it.

You can look at your "what I need" Mandala. Is there something there you find supportive, inspiring, or helpful? If so, if it were a color, which would it be? Paint a rock and then write the word that goes with that support.

Example of Support Stones

You can revisit your Tree of Strength and all the Resources on the leaves as a reminder.

Embrace these support stones. You can make more and more of them at any time, creating many Resources to have at your fingertips, literally.

TIP: It helps to have both your Tree of Strength and your Support Stones within view, to reinforce the positive within you. Let your **mirror neurons** do the work.

Spending time looking at positive, feel-good experiences allows the nervous system to take in the positive and restore resilience by matching the positive without you doing more than just looking, feeling it, and taking it in. Feels like magic, huh?!

Pick up and hold a rock, even rub it to feel its presence any time you feel you need it. Activate those mirror neurons.

F: CONCLUSION & SUPPORT WORK

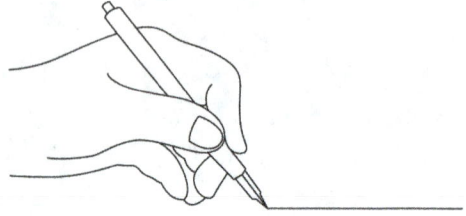

CONCLUSION:

In this chapter, we learned about resources and how they provide physical, emotional, and spiritual support.

You created a **"What you need" Mandala, Support Stones,** and had an option to participate in the **Best Self,** a guided meditation. After each exercise, you also wrote in the Workbook or your journal and drew a picture to support further and develop your resource bank.

These resources will help you in your journey to uncover and heal your **Mother Wound**.

Below are a few writing prompts to help us focus on the topic of this book.

This workbook can stand alone, and I have included supplemental reading that you may find interesting, expansive, and stimulating as you navigate through Overcoming your Mother Wound.

Below are a few prompts I suggest you answer regarding your supplemental reading.

SUPPLEMENTAL READING

Between sessions, if you are reading one of my hand-picked suggested books or something else on the subject, write below or in your journal your response to what you are reading.

Here are some questions you can use to start thinking about the book you chose:

What jumps out at you from the book? _____

_____

_____

_____

What feels new?

Does anything feel old?

What do you connect with most in the book?

What do you connect with least?

CHAPTER 4:
PENDULATE

Overcoming the Mother Wound

A: PENDULATION

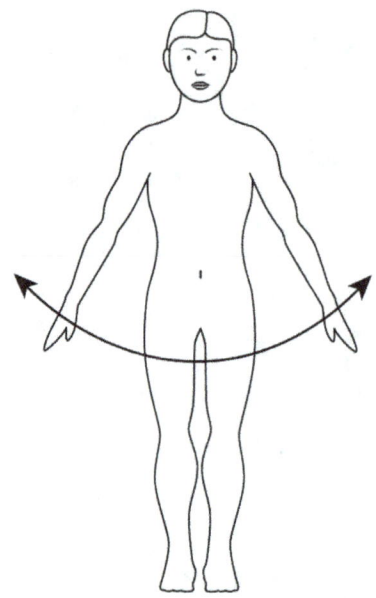

Let me explain what I mean by **Pendulate** and why it is the name of this chapter.

Pendulation is a term used in Somatic Experiencing ™, and it refers to moving from a state of calm or ease to a state of activation or distress. A state of expansion and contraction, which is what our autonomic nervous system constantly wants to do automatically.

When we "Pendulate," we tune into the natural rhythms of our body and honor where we are and what we can or cannot do. This act allows us to expand our ability to **tolerate** more: more emotion, more experience, and more clarity about ourselves.

B: WOT

Speaking of Tolerating, this brings me to the WOT, which stands for Window of Tolerance. Dan Siegal developed this term in his 1999 book "The Developing Mind" to describe the Optimal State of Arousal between the two main branches of the autonomic nervous system (sympathetic and parasympathetic).

Imagine the shape of an actual window; see below.

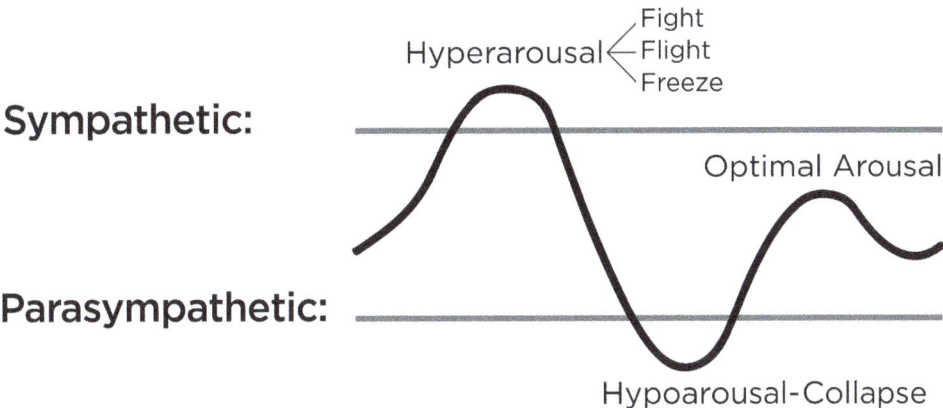

At the top of the window is the most activated your nervous system can be, and you are still within your range of tolerance without being in extreme activation or going into a state of Hyperarousal (outside the window).

Conversely, at the bottom is the most deactivated you can be without disconnecting from reality or being in a state of Hyperarousal (also outside the window).

If you look at the WOT graph, there is a space for Optimal Arousal. That space can be large or small, depending on the situation, your experiences, and your temperament.

When we Pendulate, meaning allowing ourselves to move from a state of being activated to deactivation, we build capacity for more emotion, and our body learns that it is safe to do so (if doing this without a somatic practitioner, please practice this will people and places we trust).

In this chapter, we will practice just that. Activating and deactivating our nervous system.

To start, begin with the usual settling exercises – Settling with Square Breath, Intention Setting, and I am adding a new exercise, the Unscramble.

C: UNSCRAMBLING EXERCISE

UNSCRAMBLING EXERCISE *APPENDIX O*

This simple pose helps to bring all your meridian energy into alignment (meridians are the energetic 'highways' of the body).

If you're feeling scrambled, confused, or stressed, this can bring you right back to your center!

This is also a pose that many children do intuitively.

Breathe in through the nose and out through the mouth.

Stand with feet side by side.

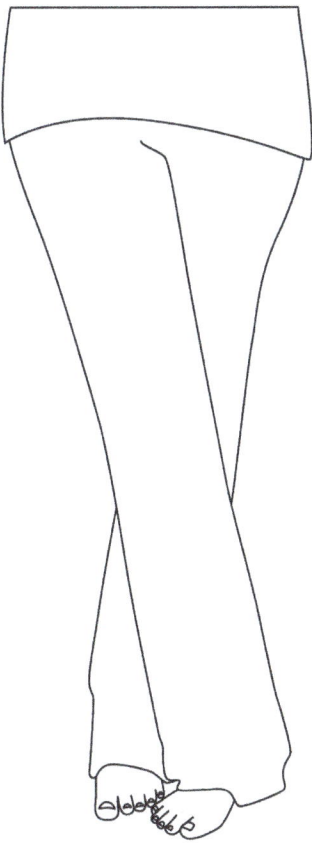

Cross one foot over the other and stand like that.

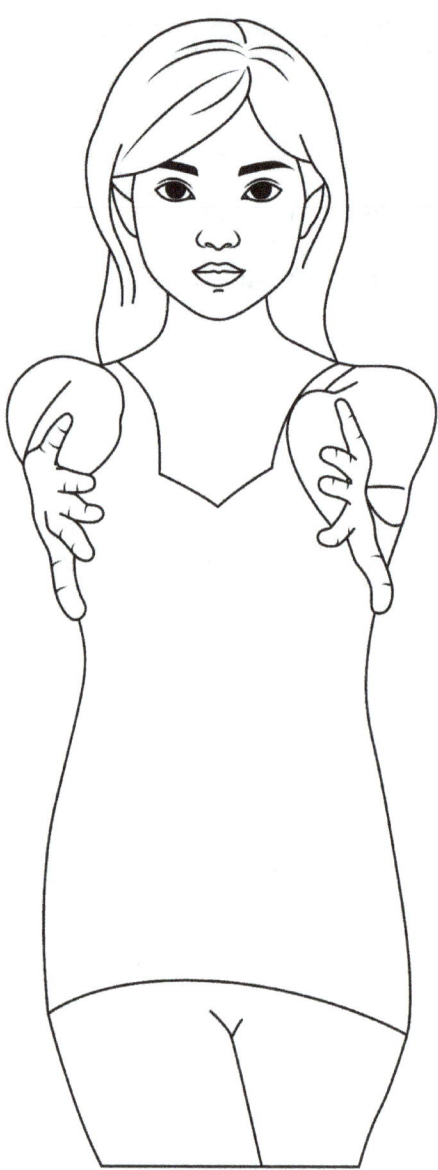

Extend your arms out in front of you, thumbs pointing down with palms facing away

Cross one arm over the other.

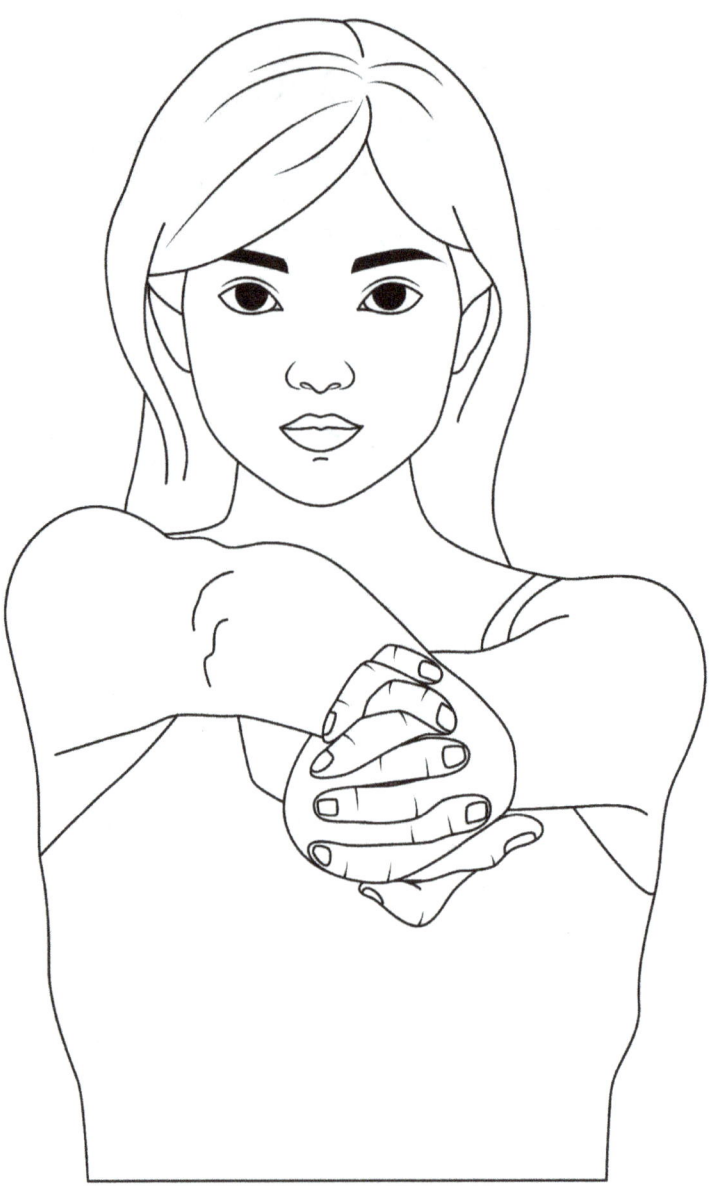

Bring the hands together, and interlace your fingers

Then scoop them up and under.

Then scoop them up and under.

MAY THIS BOOK BRING HOPE AND INSPIRATION

Your legs are crossed, and your arms are crossed.

Breathe in through the nose and out through the mouth. Repeat 3 times.

Then reverse it. Switch hands: Unhook your hands, cross the other one on top, and hook them up.

Then uncross your feet and cross the other one on top.

Breathe in through the nose and out through the mouth. Repeat this 3 times.

After the last exhale, uncross everything.

Bring your hands together over your heart as if in prayer.

Take one more breath here; bow to your day's intention.

Stand tall and shake out your hands.

How was that? Do you feel any different?

These exercises are meant to bring you more fully into your WOT.

D: WHAT WE THINK

Bring your attention to something you may have already noticed but may have dismissed or excused.

You see, as we move through this book, we may have many different thoughts, beliefs, and feelings all of the time. When we don't pay attention to them, they can take hold, whether they are accurate or not.

Below is an exercise that highlights some of what may be going on inside of you.

If we can notice and keep track of what happens internally, it is no longer "inside," and we can look at it, play with it, and share it with someone or something we trust. (A friend, therapist, pet, even a tree.)

Here are possible thoughts, feelings, and beliefs you may have, and then prompts to help you write your responses here or in your journal.

YOU MAY BELIEVE...

- YOU DON'T UNDERSTAND
- I'M MAKING PROGRESS
- I'M WORTHY
- I DESERVE SUPPORT
- THIS IS STUPID
- HEALING TAKES TIME
- THIS WILL NEVER GO AWAY
- I'M ALONE
- I CAN DO THIS
- I'M HEALING
- THIS IS UNCONSEQUENTIAL
- I'M OK

I believe Mother Wounds are _____

I am reading this book, and I believe that I will _____

I believe that if I do the exercises in this book _____

I believe that by reading this book, I am _____

I believe _____

YOU MAY FEEL...

RELIEVED　SADNESS　APATHETIC
DISCOMFORT
RESISTANT　RELAXATION　JOY
AFRAID　CONFUSION　WISE　ANGER
　　HOPEFUL　SUPPORTED
UNCERTAINTY

I feel _____ about the material in this book.

I feel _____ after making art for this book.

I feel _____ when I try the Intention Setting exercise.

I feel _____ that I am on a journey to heal my Mother Wound.

I feel _____

YOU MAY WANT TO...

RETURN TO OLD PATTERNS　DIVE IN　CALL A FRIEND
TAKE A BREAK
RUN AWAY　　SPEED UP THE PROCESS
GET DISTRACTED　KEEP GOING　LEAVE
ISOLATE　IGNORE YOUR FEELINGS　REACH OUT

When I start a new chapter, I want to _____

When I complete a chapter, I want to _____

When I do _____ exercise, I want to _____

I notice that if a lesson or exercise is _____ , I want to _____

I want to _____

Please feel free to continue writing with these prompts, expanding as much as you'd like.

Keep noting your thoughts, feelings, and beliefs below or in your journal as you move along this book.

TIP: Putting repetitive thoughts on paper helps keep them out of your mind.

E: MEDITATION RESOURCE: CALM PLACE – GUIDED MEDITATION (GM) APPENDIX E

Calm Place

Today, you will be learning a new resource through guided meditation. I call this a Resource, like I call the Best Self a "Resource," because these are internal experiences that are very real and supportive.

When you can visualize and feel a connection to a positive resource, the mind/body connection experiences this as if it is happening.

It is found that when we experience something in this mind/body connection for even a few moments, that experience becomes real on the cellular level.

Our brains make new neural connections and can even replace outdated shoddy connections. In other words, connections are no longer doing us any good.

These exercises aim to replace outdated connections with new, more positive neural pathways.

Resources, like creating support stones, help you stay longer in the positive experience, thus allowing this positive neural pathway to linger and grow.

In other words, the more you use your resources, the more you reinforce more positivity in your brain!

And what better way than through the Art Prompts, Journaling Exercises, and Guided Meditations I'm sharing with you throughout this book?

Creating change doesn't have to be boring.

You can use these Resources 24/7.

The more you use them, the stronger they get.

Let's bring in another Resource.

Below is a Meditation that can help you feel calm by creating a special place for yourself.

This place is created in your imagination, and you can access it and feel it anytime you want.

Recommendation: record the words below and then play the audio when you are in a place where you can close your eyes and listen.

When you see the word "pause," do not say the word out loud but be still and "pause" in silence.

Give yourself 10 – 20 minutes to settle, listen, and respond in writing or art-making about what you see, feel, or whatever else you experienced.

To start, find a spot where you won't be disturbed for at least 10 minutes, longer if you'd like to have time to settle before and time to reflect and even draw your experience afterward.

You can imagine this as you read, but I highly recommend recording the meditation on a device such as your phone so that it can be handy later, too. Also, we will be using this meditation throughout this book, and this way, you'll be able to come back to your calm place whenever you'd like.

Make yourself as comfortable as possible, but not so comfortable that you will fall asleep. If you do fall asleep, trust that you will still hear exactly what it is you need to hear.

When we listen to guided meditations, it is best to let go of our thinking brain and trust the unconscious is attentively listening. This way, our mind can take a break and let other, less active, but equally valuable parts of us be in charge.

Let's begin:

Start to become more aware of your breathing, noticing the rhythm, pace, and sound of the breath. *pause.*

On your next inhale, hold for a moment, then release slowly and fully.

Again, breathing in, holding, and letting go.

Continue breathing, letting the body do all the work. Letting thoughts come and go, noticing, and being. *pause.*

As you begin to relax, think of a place, real or imagined, where you feel most comfortable, most at ease, most at peace. *pause.*

This may be a place you've read about, seen in a movie, dreamed about or even been to.

Take your time and see what comes to you, *pause.*

Have you found it? *pause.*

Look around; what is there? *pause.*

What colors? *pause.*

What feelings go with this place? *pause.*

Are you outside? Are you in nature? *pause.*

Are you inside? What are there furnishings? *pause.*

What sounds do you hear? *pause.*

What time of day is it? *pause.*

What temperature? *pause.*

Is there a breeze? *pause.*

What do you smell? *pause.*

Take note and hang out in your calm place for a few moments.

After listening to or reading the meditation, here are some journal prompts for you if you'd like to take time to reflect:

How was the meditation? _____

_____

_____

I was most surprised that I was able to _____

_____

_____

My calm place reminded me of _____

_____

_____

I noticed that my calm place _____

_____

_____

_____

I was surprised that I _____

_____

_____

I want to remember _____ about my Calm Place because _____

_____

F: ART TIME - YOUR CALM PLACE ART MAKING EXPERIENCE

ART TIME

By making art after meditation, we further deepen or embody an experience. When we "embody" something, the experience becomes felt in the body, which supports the mind/body connection we seek for true change to occur. That's why I include an Art Making Experience for your Calm Place.

Drawing helps reinforce your experience by using mirror neurons and as well as supporting other healthy brain functions having to do with Neuroplasticity.

Bring up the image of your Calm Place, be there for a moment, see it, feel it.

Using colors, lines, or images, draw your Calm Place and all the feels that go with it on a piece of blank paper.

Look at your image and remember what you saw and felt in the mediation as you look at your picture.

Keep it near; feel the calm it brings. Hang out with this feeling.

Remember, with this artwork, the feeling and memory count. Not perfection.

G: CONCLUSION & SUPPORTWORK

CONCLUSION:

This chapter taught you how to **unscramble** to align your meridian energy.

You found your **Calm Place** and solidified it through an art-making exercise.

Use the "Calm Place" Resource:

Start going to your "Calm Place" when you feel the need. Remember, your Calm Place is a Resource. Bring this forward with you from now on. You can use the image from your Art Making Experience to remind you of it.

Support Stones:

Is there anything from your Calm Place experience that belongs on a Support Stone? A feeling? A scene? A sensation? If so, make another Support Stone.

The more you commit yourself to these exercises, the more you will feel their benefits.

Supplemental Reading:

Continue reading your book from the **book recommendation** list. Write any feelings, insights, or "aha moments" that arise in your journal. You can also share these insights in the OCMW Membership Community if you are a member.

Supplemental Reading Prompts:

These prompts can help you get the most out of your reading in your journal or below. You can do them again as you progress in your reading and see if your answers change or if they stay the same:

The book that I chose is _____

I chose this book because of _____

What jumps out for me in this book is _____

This book reminds me _____

This book helped me realize _____

In this book, I connect most with _____

In this book, I connect least with _____

CHAPTER 5:
DIALOGUE WITH THE CRITIC

Overcoming the
Mother Wound

A: Overview

This chapter is very experiential, meaning you will be actively experiencing this lesson rather than learning about it.

There are several parts to this chapter. We start with an art experience, then writing prompts, a two-handed dialogue, more writing prompts, an art-making project, and conclude with a resourcing exercise at the end.

This workbook will guide you step by step.

By now, however, you may feel the effects of this type of self-exploration as confusion, boredom, impatience, or glee.

You may uncover things you had forgotten about yourself and find things you are ready to let go of, such as when you did the "What You Need" Mandala exercise in Chapter Three.

Or maybe you are more aware of your knee-jerk responses from the "What We Think, Fee, Believe" exercise in Chapter Four.

There is no right or wrong here. The hope is that you begin to be more curious about the effects of a mother wound. First, we want to fortify you from the inside out and be closer to that more confident you!

These resources have all been carefully selected and are meant to support you through the content, help when things feel heavy and make it an enjoyable self-exploration with the meditations and Art Making Exercises.

FOR THIS LESSON YOU WILL NEED:

- Your Journal
- Plain paper
- 2 different colored pens or colored pencils.
- Access to your bedroom for an Art-Making Exercise, if possible. If not, it can be from memory (I'll explain!).

If you can, start with the Settling Exercise, Setting an Intention Exercise, and Unscrambling exercise found in the APPENDIXES L, M, O.

B: PART 1 - Art Making Experience

What is a little different here is that I will ask you to note **your thoughts** as you make this drawing.

Let's go:

Draw your bedroom.

Take no more than 15 minutes to draw it.

Observe your self-talk. Is there much? What is the tone? Make note of it and do your best.

Remember 5-15 minutes max to make your drawing, then flip your paper over and take 5-10 minutes max to write all the voices you heard.

These are your inner voices.

NOTE: You'll want to keep these notes handy, whether negative or positive; they will be valuable in this and in future lessons.

Here are some prompts to ponder:

I noticed _____

My negative voices were _____

While my positive voices were _____

I feel the negative voices are _____ and

the positive voices are _____

As I created my drawing, I heard mostly _____

What came to mind as I was drawing was _____

C: PART 2 – Who is the Critic

WHO IS THE CRITIC?

In this exercise, we're going to have a dialogue with the Critic, if you have one. Most people do.

What is different between us is the degree of negativity and harm inflicted on our psyche by believing our Critic. A lot also depends on our relationship with the critic.

Let's explore the critic.

Is there a voice commenting or directing? _____

What happens to you when you hear that voice? _____

How often does it show up? _____

When? _____

Where? _____

It helps to notice and even make notes of it in your journal. Heck, you might even hear a little commentator about this chapter or even the book. This is important.

We want to know better who this critic is, what makes it tick, and whether it has anything to say that is not critical or negative.

The more you notice and the more you keep a tally, the better chance you have of building a relationship with these internal voices. You may even grasp a feeling or an age that goes with those critical beliefs.

D: PART 3 - DIALOGUING

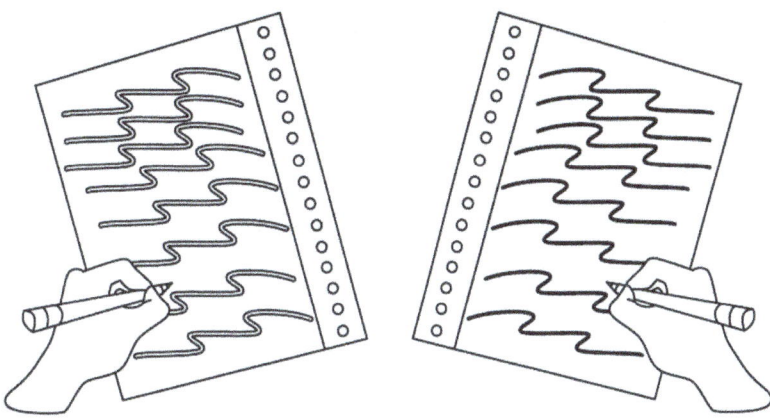

Using an unlined piece of paper and 2 different colors of writing tools, you will create a dialogue with one of the critical or negative voices you felt or heard talking to you and the noncritical part of you.

For the critic, if you need to look at your journal or your notes on the back of your drawing on what was said or how it made you feel, please do.

Take a moment first and connect with your **Calm Place**. Remember this feeling inside of you.

Next, when you are ready, connect to positive feelings you have from your **Best Self** resource.

Also, connect to any excitement, hope, or pleasure you have experienced so far in this book or elsewhere.

Once you connect to those feelings, choose a colored writing tool that matches – Color #1.

Then, hear that negative voice and how it may have sounded while you were drawing your bedroom earlier. Choose a color that matches that voice - Color #2

Now, place the part of you that has that spark of **positive feeling** (Color #1) in your dominant hand and the **commentating voice** (as you were drawing) in your non-dominant hand (Color #2).

Then, begin a dialogue. Only one voice can talk at a time.

Make sure you listen to each other, one hand at a time. This dialogue can be 10–20 minutes long.

See what emerges.

After the dialogue is complete, thank each other.

E: ART TIME 1: EXAGGERATE THE CRITIC

I'm including a couple of Art Prompts to go even deeper with this lesson:

Make a drawing of the critical voice and what it may look like if it were a thing, a color, or a shape.

Exaggerate the Critic and make it into a cartoon of itself. Play with the size and shape.

Feel what it is like to see this image on paper, separate from you.

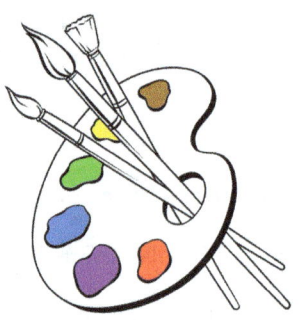

ART TIME

Follow these prompts:

I was surprised that

My critic reminded me of

My critic felt as big as

My critic felt as small as

These are the insights I'd like to share

F: ART TIME 2: CONTAIN THE CRITIC

Sometimes, we need a place to keep things that we don't need or that interfere with what we want and need, like a critical voice. Sometimes we just need some distance from those things that are interfering (think of a noisy street, and you need to close the window so it's quieter).

A container holds things that are too much at any given time.

Contain the Critic Mandala Instructions: (Sample below)

Use the image you just created, or make a new one, then place your exaggerated critic in the center of your paper.

Next, grab a drawing or coloring tool and make a big, thick circle around your "critic."

You can use a dinner plate or compass to create the circle.

This Mandala is meant to separate you from your Critic.

If you want to be fancy, place your best self, calm place and any other positive resources you can think outside the circle of your critic, to separate you from your critic.

Contain the Critic Mandala Example:

This creates a Container for the Critic.

If you enrolled in an Overcoming the Mother Wound Course be sure to share it in the Membership Group. (See link to join in Appendix J)

G: CONCLUSION & SUPPORT WORK

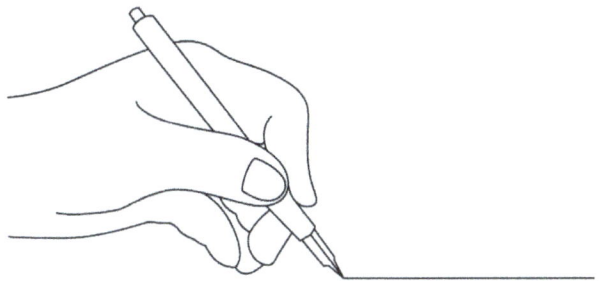

CONCLUSION:

In this chapter, you discovered your inner voices and learned how to separate positive and negative voices to identify the **Critic**.

You created a dialogue with the Critic and used an art-making experience to gain more insight on interacting with them.

SUPPORT WORK:

Your support work for this module is to check in on your resources. In the morning, before you go to sleep, at lunchtime, at art time, or at any time

Use the "Calm Place" Resource:

Start going to your "Calm Place" when you feel the need. You can use your Art Making Experience image to remind you of it.

Calm Place

Supplemental Reading:

Continue reading your book from the recommended book list found in the Appendix. Write any feelings, insights, or "Aha's" that come up in your journal. Drop me a note in the OCMW Facebook group: https://www.facebook.com/groups/overcomingthemotherwound

CHAPTER 6: SELF-ACCEPTANCE AND RESOURCING

Overcoming the Mother Wound

A: OVERVIEW & PRE-WORK

We are at the halfway mark of this workbook.

You may notice that we repeat exercises and reinforce lessons with art, which may take longer than you expected.

If these are your thoughts, you are correct. It has been found that the best way to learn is through repetition. It has also been found that to heal a Mother Wound, we must repeat and reinforce what we are learning, not just in words, but non-verbally, i.e., using the creative process, whether that is making art, writing, movement, or guided meditation.

We call this the "Bottom Up" approach (feeling it then knowing it) versus "Top Down" (learning it through cognition and telling the body it is so).

Have you been remembering to call on your Resources?

As an assist, I'm listing the resources you've gathered so far:

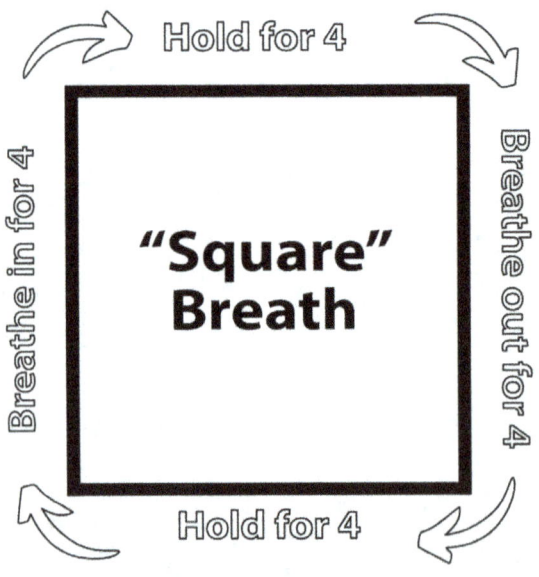

MAY THIS BOOK BRING HOPE AND INSPIRATION

Tree of Strength

These resources and your journaling, artmaking, and supplemental reading are meant to support you along this workbook's journey.

The resources are here to offer you tools and ways to navigate any arising emotions, either for reflection or for potential healing.

In this chapter, we are going to learn another resource, but before we do that, we'll start like we do every session, with a check-in, Settling Exercise, Intention Setting, and Unscrambling before I give you a scripted meditation and accompanying Art prompt so that you can create and journal for this lesson.

FOR THIS LESSON YOU WILL NEED:

- Uninterrupted time, if possible.
- Your journal.
- A blank piece of paper, pencils, pens, and markers.

SUPPORT EXERCISES:

We will start with our Settling, Intention Setting, and Unscrambling exercises. To help you remember:

Settling Exercise ***APPENDIX L***

Setting an Intention Exercise ***APPENDIX M***

Unscrambling Exercise ***APPENDIX O***

Now that you are feeling settled, have your intention, and are unscrambled, let's go further.

B: RESOURCING AND SELF-ACCEPTANCE

Today, we will do some resourcing and self-acceptance work through art and our imagination before our deeper dive into some tougher terrain.

Resourcing in this book is building on supporting the best parts of you, so you can build more positive memories in your brain and create new neural networks to hold these positive experiences—a win-win for heart and head healing.

Self-acceptance is curiosity about who we are and learning how we feel about our different parts.

Is there a grump in the house? A hungry part? Thirsty part? Sleepy one? Hurt part? Is there an eager part?

Can't wait for the next lesson already?

Maybe there is a shining star part that's in the shadows? You won't know until we find out.

C: MEDITATION RESOURCE: YOUR ANIMAL (APPENDIX C)

YOUR ANIMAL

Here is another guided meditation that I have written, and I recommend you record it so you can have it handy and listen whenever you'd like.

Or have someone you love record it for you.

When you see the word "pause," do not say the word out loud but be still and "pause" in silence.

Give yourself 10 – 20 minutes to settle, listen, and respond in writing or art-making about what you see, feel, or whatever else you experienced.

When you are ready, find yourself in a quiet spot where you will not be interrupted or disturbed to listen to this brief and gentle guided meditation and see what animal is revealed to you:

About your animal resource:

This is not an animal you know or that you've seen. It has no name.

Here is your **ANIMAL MEDITATION RESOURCE:**

Find a comfortable place to be, and sit in a comfortable spot.

A place where you can feel the support of the ground or floor beneath you, where your back is supported, and you are comfortable.

Begin to notice your breathing…., in…, out, breathing in and breathing out, noticing if the breath is fast, slow, that's it, allow the breath to come into your chest, into your belly, and then release and let go.

Feel the rhythm of your breathing, breathing deeper and deeper, as you feel the support beneath you, the space around you, letting sounds filter through you, letting any sensations come and go.

Letting any thoughts come and go.

As the body relaxes, the noises in the brain can get louder; that's what the brain does, allow them to come and go, let the noise come and go, turning down the dial just for a few moments, that's it, keeping the volume low, paying attention to your breathing, *pause*.

And when you feel even more comfortable, I want you to bring up an ANIMAL.

This is not an animal you have ANY relation with or have seen somewhere and know it by name.

Let this animal come to you; let it appear.

There is no right or wrong animal; see what is there and what wants to come forth.

When your animal has arrived, look into its eyes and let it look into yours, *pause*.

Tilt your forehead towards each other, looking into each other's eyes, *pause*.

Does your animal have a scent? Is your animal making any sounds?

Standing with your animal, reach out and touch the surface of your animal and feel its texture.

pause.

Gently put your hand over your animal's heart, feel the heart beating, and allow your animal to put a hand over your heart.

Feel each other's hearts beating, *pause*.

Let your animal know you see it, that you feel it. *pause*.

Let your animal know you know it is there, and the animal let you know it is here for you.

pause.

We're coming back now.

Slowly begin to breathe a little deeper, become aware of your belly rising, your chest rising, the sensation of breath coming in and out.

Become aware of the ground beneath you, the surface supporting you; start to wiggle your fingers, your toes, your wrists, your ankles; begin to stretch and move your body, fluttering your eyes open.

Look around the room, noticing what is in your environment.

Rub your palms on your thighs. Come back, come back, you're back.

Drink a glass of water, make sure you are awake and alert!

D: MEET YOUR ANIMAL - JOURNALING AND ART-MAKING EXERCISE TO TAKE IT FURTHER

You can take this further by writing about the meditation in your journal.

Here are some prompts to get you started:

This guided meditation made me feel

My Animal appeared when

My Animal is

I was surprised that

How did it feel to connect with your animal if you did?

E: ART TIME: MEET YOUR ANIMAL

ART TIME

A great way to enhance this meditation is to draw your animal or your best representation of your animal inside of a circle (a Mandala).

Remember, we are building and strengthening new positive neural networks by engaging in something that feels supportive.

Drawing your Animal is a great way to strengthen the sense of connection between you and your Animal; this also keeps your Animal with you for the subsequent lessons and beyond.

I'll be referring you back to your Animal, Best Self, and your Calm Place. It's great to have a physical representation of them to keep with you. Both are Resources intended to support you with the material in this book.

F: CONCLUSION & SUPPORT WORK

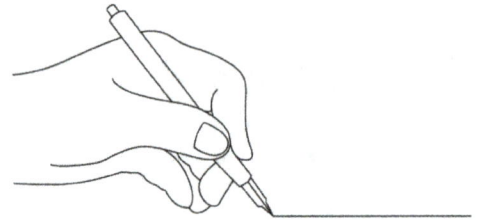

CONCLUSION:

In this chapter, you met your **Animal** and solidified its presence through artmaking and journaling.

You created an animal Mandala for your resource bank and to further enhance neuroplasticity.

Reminder:

You can bring the characteristics of your Best Self, Calm Place, or Animal with you at any time, especially when doing your homework!

Create an Animal Mandala:

During your work on this lesson, spend more time with your Animal by creating a new Mandala.

This one is your **Animal Mandala.** That's right, have another circle handy. Bring up your Animal, the image, the feeling; even look at the one you may have already drawn.

Let's put this Animal inside the circle. See what colors go with it, see if anything else wants to go inside this circle. See if anything needs to go outside the circle. I think you may be getting a handle on these Mandalas.

Are they helping? What are you experiencing? Please share.

These Mandalas are _____

What really helps is _____

I don't want to share because _____

Use your resources!

The "Calm Place" Resource:

Start going to your "Calm Place" when you feel the need. Bring this forward with you from now on.

Use your Art Time experience images to remind you of it.

Make More Resources as Desired:

Create more Support Stones, keep your Animal nearby, or make more Mandalas.

Call on any of the resources that feel supportive to you at any time that you feel you can use them.

Keep in mind you are building and supporting new neural pathways with positive thoughts, feelings, and actions.

Suggested Reading:

Are there any parallels between what you've learned about yourself here and what you are learning in your book? _____

The book I chose is _____, and it is reinforcing that I _____

The Aha's I've noticed are _____

CHAPTER 7:
MOTHER WOUND – SOLAR PLEXUS CHAKRA

Overcoming the Mother Wound

A: OVERVIEW & PRE-WORK

You are well into this workbook. How is it going?

Imagine having a conversation with me or some non-judgmental person. What would you want to tell me, or them, about how you are navigating the Mother Wound material?

_____
_____
_____
_____
_____
_____
_____
_____
_____
_____
_____
_____
_____
_____

You made it to Chapter 7, which means you are making great progressing in the book. So brave!

We've dipped into some gentle and some not-so-gentle waters of experience. Thank you for bringing your open mind and heart to every experience in whatever way you can.

FOR THIS LESSON, YOU WILL NEED:

- Uninterrupted time, if possible, for a guided meditation.
- Your Journal.
- Your art-making tools, such as paper, pens, or crayons.

B: SUPPORT EXERCISES:

We will start with our Settling, Intention Setting, and Unscrambling exercises. To help you remember:

Settling Exercise ***APPENDIX L***

Setting an Intention Exercise ***APPENDIX M***

Unscrambling Exercise ***APPENDIX O***

Now that you are feeling settled, have your intention, and are unscrambled, let's go further.

Okay, ready to work?

C: CHAKRAS

This chapter and the next work we do is with the Solar Plexus Chakra, part of the Energy System of the Chakra. Chakra (cakra in Sanskrit) means "wheel" and refers to different energy points in your body.

The Chakras are part of a belief system about physiology and the psyche that came from Indian traditions. The belief is that human life simultaneously exists in two parallel dimensions, one "physical body" and a "subtle body." The subtle body is energy, while the physical body is mass.

The belief is that the body and the mind mutually affect each other The subtle body consists of energy channels connected by nodes of psychic energy called chakras.

There was a Hindu author and sage, Patanjali, who compiled and synthesized ancient knowledge of Sanskrit works and created The Yoga Sutras about the theory and practice of Yoga.

According to Patanjali's Yoga Sutra, the body has 7 main Chakras or energy centers inside the body—the Root, Sacral, Solar Plexus, Heart, Throat, Third Eye, and Crown. They are arranged in a column along the spinal cord, from its base to the top of the head, connected by vertical channels.

According to Dr. Sri Amit Ray, who is a meditation master and philosopher and currently teaches on peace, non-violence, compassion, and mindful AI, there are 114 chakras in the human body.

These are split into 7 major chakras, 21 minor chakras, and 86 micro chakras.

Chakras, or wheels, have ancient origins in the Hindu and Buddhist traditions, and their etymology can also be traced to ancient Greece.

This mediation will focus on the Solar Plexus, the 3rd Chakra, located below the chest and above the belly button, indicated by the color yellow. It is said to be our power center, where we can feel a sense of Self.

Let's get started.

D: EXPLORING THE MOTHER WOUND. THE SOLAR PLEXUS GUIDED MEDITATION (APPENDIX F)

Start by making yourself comfortable, lying down, or sitting up.

Ensure you won't be disturbed for 10-20 minutes.

Have your journal and/or drawing materials nearby for the exercise portion of today's lesson.

REMINDER: Throughout the book, I reference boys/girls, daughters/sons, and he/she interchangeably as we refer to the mother wound.

When you are ready, read and record this brief meditative transmission, then relax and listen to it:

When you see the word "pause," do not say the word out loud but be still and "pause" in silence.

We all have chakras, energy centers in our bodies, and we are going to focus on the solar chakra just above your belly button.

Start by sitting upright or lying on your back.

Close your eyes, and take a deep breath in, and inhale through the entire center of your body, especially your belly.

Hold the breath there for just a moment, then focus your energy around your navel, *pause,* and slowly exhale, allowing your belly button to sink towards your spine as you let your breath out.

We are connecting to our energy center, our life force, the area that holds the memory of the cord that connected us in our mother's womb, *pause.*

Our life growing inside of her. Our body living in hers. Here is the Solar Plexus Chakra, associated with our sense of self, our sense of aliveness and identity, and connected to our experiences with our mothers.

The mother wound is a trauma handed down from mother to child, *pause.*

Often, the mother has experienced her own disillusionments and traumas and unconsciously carries her experiences of loss, rage, neglect, abuse, unfulfilled dreams, and grief deep in their psyche.

Passing down through the generations unresolved pain and sorrow to future generations, *pause.*

Notice what is coming up for you.

Take note of your thoughts, feelings, and bodily sensations.

Then begin to breath deeper and deeper, becoming aware of the weight of your body, start wiggling your toes and your fingers, flutter your eyes open.

Stretch if you need to, and grab a glass of water. You may be moving some energy as you feel and experience things related to your mother wound.

No worries, this is only energy, and it just wants to move. A natural, healthy response when we are learning and growing

E: ART TIME: SOLAR PLEXUS ART-MAKING EXPERIENCE

ART TIME

The Solar Chakra Meditation can bring up inner material you may not always access. This makes it a great time for art making. Art supports the unconscious and gives it a voice.

With your art-making supplies at the ready, think about what a mother wound means to you.

How would *you* describe it in the context of your own childhood environment?

Make a sketch – in words or images of feelings or memories. Use any colors or materials you would like.

If you would rather, you can describe your mother below in the comments or in your journal.

My mother is/was _____

_____

_____

_____

My relationship with my mother is/was _____

_____

_____

_____

F: CONCLUSION & SUPPORT WORK

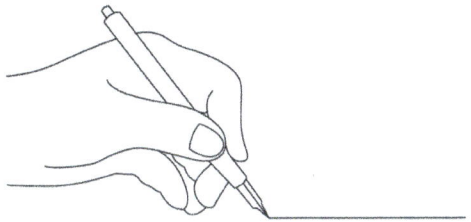

CONCLUSION:

The guided meditation centered on the Solar Plexus, the third Chakra in the body and the place where we can best feel a sense of Self.

The art-making experience helped you explore the Solar Plexus Chakra some more, and now the "What's in my Control Mandala" is to help focus your attention and intentions.

Example of Support Stones

Support Stones:

Read, draw, and rub your support stones. Do what you need to feel resourced.

Use Your Resources:

Go back to any of the meditations, "Best Self," "Calm Place," or "Mother Wound and Solar Plexus Exploration," and listen again.

When you are done listening, I invite you to draw your feelings about it or journal.

What's in My Control Mandala:

Remember Mandalas? Good, we're going to **make a new one**.

Like the "What I Need" Mandala" (sample below)

This one is the "What's in my Control Mandala."

Example of What I want near

The "**What's in My Control Mandala**" will use the inside to separate things from the outside.

Let me explain:

We use images, words, and colors to make this Mandala.

On the inside, put the things you can control or do something about, and on the outside, put the things you cannot control (other people, the color of your eyes).

Remember to **thicken** the line around your Mandala if you would like it to feel stronger and more separate, being sure to keep some things on the outside of the circle out.

Notice, too, how close the things you want to keep in or leave out are to the line of the Mandala.

Continue this exercise throughout the book and beyond, as needed.

Mandalas can be supportive, a way to focus your attention and intention and separate what is most significant for you now.

Explore in your journal:

Is your self-talk changing?

Is it getting easier to ask for what you need and to let go of what you don't?

Suggested Reading:

Continue reading your book from the suggested reading list.

How is it going?

Any surprises?

Do you find you want to skip or skim? Return? _____

Are you reading the same sentence again and again? _____

Keep writing any feelings, insights, or "aha moments" that come up here or in your journal _____

Images of your Support Stones, Mandalas, or other artwork are also welcome in the OCMW Facebook group: https://www.facebook.com/groups/overcomingthemotherwound

CHAPTER 8: TYPES OF MOTHER WOUND

Overcoming the Mother Wound

A: OVERVIEW & PRE-WORK

How are you? Ready for an even deeper dive?

Before we start:

Take a look at your Tree of Strength from Chapter 1 and choose a word or two from a "leaf" and feel this part of you.

Tree of Strength

Choose a stone to be a support stone. Now set these aside, they will be part of your homework.

Support Stones

At this point, you could be feeling anything from liberated to frustrated. This is important work you are doing. Letting in all feelings and experiences can be a great growth experience. If it is too much, please trust your limits.

Remember your Keep In/Out Mandala? The circle that you put the images and words you want to keep near inside your Mandala and the words and images you want to keep at a distance outside the Mandala's circle?

Let your mirror neurons absorb what it is you want to keep near and what you do not. Let your brain do the work. All you need to do is look at your mandala and see what it is you want.

The mother wound can leave such an imprint, especially for daughters and sons of critical or unavailable mothers.

Bringing awareness to this, using the Resources, the artmaking, journaling, Support Stones, and guided meditations are here to support your choice to look at this wound and provide ways for you to explore healing it.

Are you ready for an even deeper dive?

Remember, go at your own pace. It's perfectly fine to return to an earlier chapter or exercise and do it again whenever you need more support before continuing.

As I said in the beginning. For some, this pace will feel fine; for others, it will feel too fast, and for others slow.

We are all different and will experience the book differently. Each of our Mother Wounds is unique and deserves our attention as such!

FOR THIS LESSON YOU WILL NEED:

- Uninterrupted time, if possible.
- Your art-making supplies.
- Your journal.

B: SUPPORT EXERCISES:

We will start with our Settling, Intention Setting, and Unscrambling exercises. To help you remember:

Settling Exercise *APPENDIX L*

Setting an Intention Exercise *APPENDIX M*

Unscrambling Exercise *APPENDIX O*

Now that you practiced settling, made your intention, and unscrambled, let's go further.

Okay, ready to work?

C: GUIDED MEDITATION: TYPES OF MOTHER WOUNDS (APPENDIX G)

Wonderful. Now, let's make sure you have the following available:

Calm Place

Your Animal

Your Best Self.

Hang out with them for a few. Gather your art materials and journal.

Find a comfortable place to sit or lie where you will not be disturbed for a good 20 minutes or so, so you read or listen to the mother wound exploration and respond afterward.

Below is the written meditation, please read and record it and listen when you are in a place where you will not be disturbed for at least 15 minutes:

When you see the word pause do not read the word out loud but be still and "pause" in silence.

Welcome to the Types of Mother Wounds Guided Meditation.

Please allow yourself to take in only what you need for today, knowing you can come back at any time to listen and receive what you need when you need it.

In case we have not had an ideal or rather a good enough, early relationship with our early caretakers, we develop wounds.

Attachment theorists refer to wounds by styles such as avoidant, ambivalent, and disorganized.

After listening to these types of wounds, you can sense into which ones resonate with you. It's not uncommon to have more than one experience with our early caretakers. Let's go a little deeper into the mother wound.

The thing about this wound is we can't see it or touch it with our hands, and yet it is there. It is here. Each wound is unique, as each child is unique, as each mother-child relationship is unique.

So, let's slow down. Give this some time, some space. If you need to take a break at any time, please do.

This guided meditation is not meant to overwhelm you, and if that is happening, please pause or bring one of your resources with you.

If you're still here, let's begin.

Start by noticing the surface you're sitting on.

Noticing how your feet are meeting the ground.

Notice your breath.

Allow any sounds or smells around you to be there, giving space to whatever needs to be there.

Coming all the way inside, following your breath as you inhale, sensing your throat, chest, stomach, belly, and as you exhale, allowing your hips to soften and spread. Feeling the weight of your legs and feet.

Breathing in and breathing out. Breathing in and breathing out.

Now, recalling our meditation with your belly, your navel chakra, just above your belly button, take a deep inhale, hold the breath there for just a moment, feeling the energy in your navel, and exhale.

Slowly dropping your navel toward your spine as you release your breath.

We are connecting with your navel energy, the center of your life force.

The memory of the cord in the womb that connected us to our mothers.

The cord that's been physically disconnected a long time ago, yet the connection lingers.

The navel center is associated with our sense of self, with our deepest sense of aliveness and security. Self, with a capital S.

The mother connection is handed down from mother to child, generation to generation.

What is your connection? *pause*

Is there love? *pause*

Hurt? *pause*

Rage? *pause*

All that and more? Less?

Many children and many adults have many different experiences with this connection. And all children and adults have this connection. What is yours?

No matter your mother's intention, what was your experience with your mother?

Here are six primary wounds a mother can pass down to a boy or girl child.

Critical mother. The critical mother wound. Was she the critical mother? No matter what you did or do for this mother it is never enough or it is too much. You are too loud or too quiet, too sensitive or too strong.

You're either too much or not enough. She attacks you for being you. This message teaches you to hate herself, and with an internal belief I am defective

This child loses their voice and their joy in order to survive. They learn It is not safe to be themselves.

The critical mother can be physically and or verbally cruel. She may craftily manipulate you with her words or outright yell and beat you. Her tone may be maternal but her message is sharp and cold.

Giving you the pain of her own hidden wounds of loss, regret, and hopelessness that she is unable to accept and own.

The child of the critical mother may live with fear and anger towards themselves and others.

Living in a negative loop unbeknownst to themselves.

The next wound is the Invisible mother.

When there is an **Invisible** mother, the child is left to their own resources and learns to fend for themselves. Turning inward to their inner world, hoping to meet their own needs in relationships where others could not.

The invisible mother births an unmothered child.

This mother may be ill, deceased or not physically present and not available to her child's needs.

If withholding of love and attention towards her child is intentional, as in the critical mother, the child experiences emotional abuse.

The child gets the message, I'm not important, I don't matter, no one can see me. When the child absorbs and believes this message, anxiety, depression, and other self-destructive or addictive behaviors develop over time.

A physically present but emotionally absent mother incurs a wound on the child. This is another form of the invisible mother wound.

Imagine a well-intending mother attending to her child's basic needs but unable to connect with the child's emotional needs. Here, the mother wound is indirect, most likely due to the child's mother's mother wound and their lack of attunement. This is a wound to the psyche, not easy to see, confusing, and painful.

The pain is even greater if the child witnesses the mother making an emotional connection with another sibling, close relatives or friends.

When a mother wound is fuzzy and unclear, it is not as quick to identify.

This wound takes patience, tenderness, and time to heal.

Even if the mother tries her best, it is a wound.

Next, the **Engulfing** mother wound. An engulfing mother may be physically overwhelming toward her child, ignoring or intruding on her personal space and in some way keeping her from experiencing the world in her own way.

The engulfing mother wants to control her child. Burdening her child with her own needs, the child of an engulfing mother finds it hard to feel who they are, what they want, believe, or need. Especially if their needs are other than their mother's expectations of them.

This child will usually either merge and stay near mother or move far away in adulthood in an attempt to feel separate and free.

It is hard for this child to simply be and develop into who that are on the inside. They often feel trapped so if they leave it's as if they escape, physically, from their mother. Without working through their wound they can be very controlling about their space, feelings, and time.

Now let's look at the **Big Little Man.** This child quickly learns that their role is to help others.

The more they give, the less they need.

The mother values her child's generosity, and over time, they become a sounding board for her inner thoughts and worries.

As the child ages, they find it harder and harder to know their own thoughts and feelings, fearing if they have their own needs, they will disappoint others.

Then we have the **Tough Guy.** The TOUGH GUY is similar to the BIG LITTLE MAN, but feel the difference between those types of wounds.

Social norms, traditions, and expectations treat boys differently than girls. Girls are generally considered more fragile, sensitive, and needy. Boys are thought to be rough, tough, loud, and dirty. Boys don't cry; boys are strong. To be vulnerable is to be a sissy.

We know **so** much more now, but cultures and even our unconscious biases may not have caught up.

The Tough Guy mother wound touches the heart of the masculine and is also seen in women.

Their genuine, generous heart that steps up when there is a need.

Here, the mother unwittingly, sometimes maliciously, takes advantage of that "tough guy" spirit.

Even requires it overtly and, more commonly, covertly.

This child learns that their role is to take care of others, override their own needs, physical and emotional, and be there for mom, the family, and others with little regard for themselves.

Not to be forgotten is the **Abandoned One** Mother Wound.

This wound grows out of the child being given mixed messages.

Being promised one thing and being given another thing or nothing at all.

Or being showered with attention in public and then ignored in private, or vice versa, creating an internal belief that **I am dispensable, I don't matter, I don't make sense, and I am ineffective**.

Pause

So, let's just take a little time to take in this information and see what resonates, see what makes sense, what feels afar, what feels close, and just let it all sift in and sift out.

Pause

Take in what you want from this experience and leave whatever you want to leave behind, behind.

Pause

We are going to be slowly coming back out of this guided meditation.

Pause

Become aware of your body being supported and becoming aware of your breathing.

Become aware of any sounds around your space.

Become aware of the temperature of the space you are in.

Feel the weight of your body.

Become aware of your breathing.

Flutter your eyes open, look around the room you are in.

Bring your hands together as if in prayer, and rub them together very quickly, stimulating the nerve in your fingers, and helping you become even more and more alert.

Take a couple of sips of air, drink some water, tap your shoulders, tap your chest, tap the top of your head, and really make sure you are back.

Then return to your workbook or journal and complete the accompanying prompts.

D: ART TIME: MOTHER WOUND JOURNALING AND ART-MAKING EXERCISE

How was that?

Take a few moments and respond to these prompts:

I identify with _____ Mother Wound(s) because

_____

I have the sensation of _____

I saw images of _____

I notice feelings of _____

I thought of _____

Please note any other thoughts, feelings, sensations, and images that came up during this meditation in your journal or in the space below.

E: MOTHER WOUNDS

After following the meditation, do you have a sense of which Mother Wound you may carry?

Similar to the four main Attachment Styles, there are six main types of Mother Wounds. You can have one, two, or a combination of more. Below is an easy reference to the types of Mother Wounds, how they develop, and case vignettes to illustrate.

Here is a breakdown of the main Mother Wounds. I have separated Men's and Women's, but I **suggest you study both**, as there they both may apply to you. See below:

FOR WOMEN:

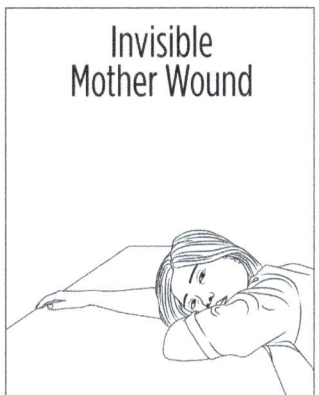

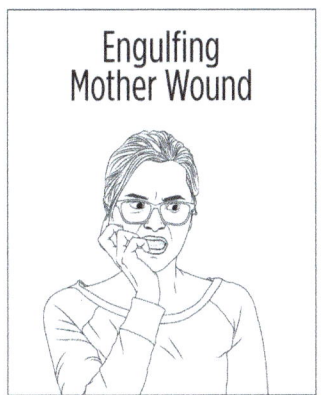

FOR MEN:

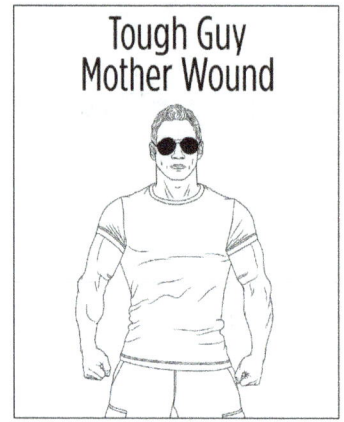

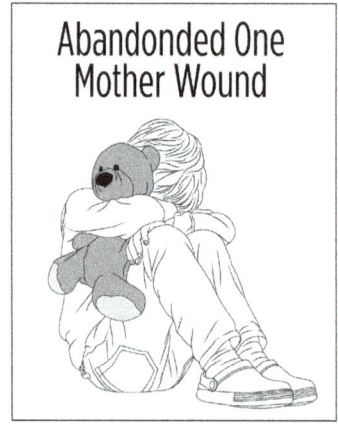

Take your time to see which, if any, resonates with you and your experience.

Take A Closer Look.

WOMEN:

CRITICAL

This Mother Wound shows up in the internal belief that no matter what I do, it will be too much or too little.

Critical Mother Wound: Daughters of a critical mother grow to believe that no matter what they do, they're too much or too little. Too loud or too lazy. Too big or too small. Too quiet or too ambitious. The resulting Mother Wound is one of deficiency, commonly manifesting from an Ambivalent/Anxious Attachment Style. Dominated by an inner critic, they move through the world, paralyzed by perfectionism. The daughter sees herself as defective and feels unsafe to be themselves. As a result, they struggle to foster and maintain secure relationships.

CRITICAL MOTHER

The CRITICAL MOTHER can happen to any child, regardless of gender. She can be physically and or verbally abusive. She may scream and yell or silently attack, using words in a polite or maternal tone while jealous or resentful of you, projecting her own wound onto her child.

Her manner can be aggressive or passive and still be relentlessly, ruthlessly critical. Unknowingly this child learns to attack herself with self-doubt, criticizing, analyzing, or dismissing her accomplishments. He or she may find the mother's critical voice in coworkers, friends, partners, and in toxic relationships. He/she/they may feel like the victim or, alternatively, try to dominate or suffer from a lack of boundaries.

The child of the **CRITICAL MOTHER** may live with fear and anger towards self and or others. Living blindly in a negative loop.

Case Vignette:

Mothering Experience:

An anxious mother and an absent father raised Gina. The family lived in a neighborhood they could not afford; Dad was overworking to make ends meet, and Mother was determined to live in a prestigious zip code and criticize those who did not. Jodi struggled to make friends; she did not wear the same clothes as others or travel to the same places. When this made her sad, her mother would tell her that it was nonsense, she is too selfish, and that she lived in a wonderful area and someday will appreciate what that meant. It would help if she tried harder and fixed her hair.

Adult:

Gina is a bright, fast-talking 29-year-old who has been in and out of therapy since her teens. She suffers from insomnia, bulimia, and an inability to orgasm. She works 12-hour days and never feels she has done enough. She once fell deeply in love in her late teens, but when he left her for the popular cheerleader, she shut down and has yet to be in another relationship.

A Critical mother wound tends to breed an Anxious Attachment Style.

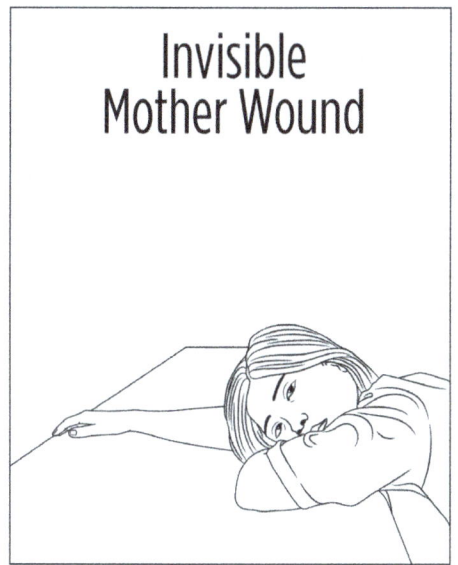

INVISIBLE (absent)

This Mother Wound shows up in the internal belief that I am not important, I am not seen, and I am left to deal with my pain alone.

Invisible Mother Wound: Daughters of an invisible or absent mother are burdened by the belief that they are alone, not seen, and not important to those around them. In the early stages of life, the daughter is left to fend for her own resources, whether physical or emotional. This type of Mother Wound often stems from developing an Avoidant Attachment Style.

In response to the neglect, the daughter turns inward to her inner world, putting up walls and struggling to let in feelings of love later in life. Despite an outward appearance of self-sufficiency, her unmet needs lead to a sense of longing.

INVISIBLE MOTHER

When there is an invisible mother, the young child is left to her own resources and learns to fend for herself. She likely turns inward to her inner world, hoping to meet her own needs in relationships where others could not. This grip is strong. He or she may avoid relationships or overcompensate in relationships for fear of that sense of nothingness experienced in childhood. With an INVISIBLE MOTHER wound, this child always reaches for his or her missing mother, unconsciously seeking her love in all situations.

The INVISIBLE MOTHER births an unmothered child. This mother may be ill, deceased, or not physically present and unavailable for her child's needs. If withholding of love and attention towards her child is intentional, as in an ATTACKING MOTHER, the child experiences emotional abuse.

She gets the message that I'm not important, I don't matter, no one can see me. When the child absorbs and believes this message, later in life, she may experience anxiety, depression, and other self-destructive or addictive behaviors. Not knowing how to self-soothe, she cries to feel alive, to be seen, felt, and heard. She seeks the love and guidance she never got, not yet knowing how to give it to herself.

The **physically present** INVISIBLE MOTHER is **emotionally** absent. Imagine a well-intending mother, attending to her child's basic needs but unable to connect and attune to her deeper needs.

Here the mother wound is indirect, most likely due to her own mother's mother wound. This is a wound to the psyche, not easy to see. Confusing and painful. This pain is even greater if the mother made a connection with another sibling.

When the mother wound is indirect or unintentional, it is not as clear-cut. Even if the mother tries her best, it is a wound. This wound takes patience, tenderness, and discernment to name. It is in this process that we find healing.

Mother may have been ill, away, deceased, dissociated, self-involved, or NOT THERE in a meaningful and consistent way.

Here is an example of an Adult with an Invisible Mothering Experience:

Kim, 43, lives alone and works at a job she now hates. She spends her weekends with friends she believes don't understand or care about her and lovers that she says are too needy. She considers moving nearer to her elderly mother but has continued to prioritize work instead.

An Invisible mother wound tends to breed an Avoidant Attachment Style.

ENGULFING (overbearing)

This type of Mother Wound shows up in the internal belief that others' needs come before I can take care of my own.

Engulfing Mother Wound: Daughters of an Engulfing Mother tend to believe that their needs and desires are secondary to those around them. The Engulfing Mother seeks to control rather than care, overwhelming their daughter with their own needs. The resulting wound is one of confusion and timidness, and the daughter finds it hard to know herself, her role, and the intentions of those around her.

This type of Mother Wound often shows up from having had a Disorganized Attachment Style with her mother. In response to a blurring of boundaries in childhood, the daughter struggles to feel trust, including in herself.

ENGULFING MOTHER

An ENGULFING MOTHER may be physically overbearing toward her child, ignoring or intruding on her personal space and in some way keeping her from experiencing the world in her own way.

The ENGULFING MOTHER wants to control her child. Overwhelming her daughter or son with her own needs. The child of an ENGULFING MOTHER finds it hard to feel who she is, what she wants, believes, or needs, especially if her needs are OTHER than her mother's expectations of her.

The child learns to believe she or he is supposed to take care of the mother instead of the mother taking care of him or her.

The ENGULFING MOTHER may overlap with the **CRITICAL MOTHER** when verbally or physically abusive.

This child is not allowed simply to be and to grow.

Instead of feeling free, she feels trapped and may physically escape her mother when she grows up, becoming territorial about her space, feelings, and time.

Mothering Experience:

Gladys is a second-generation immigrant from abroad. Her mother never tried to learn English, depending on Gladys to explain or do things for her. Gladys admits that when she was little, this made her feel special and valuable, but their relationship was transactional – you do this for me, and I will give you that - and if Gladys did not comply, she would be beaten with a belt. She felt obligated but angry at the same time, guilty and confused for having these feelings.

Adult:

Gladys is a 37-year-old working professional. She keeps gaining more and more certificates in her field with the expectation of promotions at her job. Instead, she is seen as the "go-to" person at work, meaning any grunt work gets piled on her full schedule. She is bitterly resentful later, but at the time, she smiles and feels seen, wanted, and appreciated.

The Engulfing Mother Wound usually develops into a Disorganized Attachment Style.

MEN:

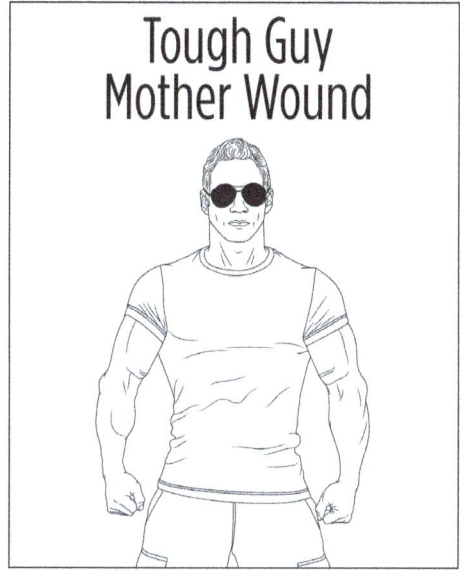

The TOUGH GUY Mother Wound develops over time and shows up in the belief that you are **the only one that can do it, and to do so, cut off feelings, even from yourself.**

Traditionally, girls are treated differently than boys; girls are thought of as being more fragile, sensitive, and needy. At the same time, boys are considered rough, tough, and strong. Boys don't cry, boys are strong. To be vulnerable is to be a sissy.

We now know this is false, but tradition lingers in our psyche. A boy crying when he scrapes his knee is fine when under the age of 5, and then it becomes less acceptable. No one may say something, but there is an air of unacceptability depending on who you are with and where you are.

Boys, *people*, are sensitive beings. Somehow boys are expected to be different. We've made huge advances with tolerance and acceptance, but my sense is that an expectation lingers.

Boys struggle to be vulnerable – women can too, don't get me wrong – but we forget the layers men endure. Sometimes unspoken and sometimes not.

We know **so** much more now, but societies, cultures, and even our unconscious biases may not have caught up.

The **TOUGH GUY** is like the BIG LITTLE MAN but feel into the difference:

The TOUGH GUY mother wound touches the heart of the masculine. His genuine, generous heart that steps up when there is a need. Here, the mother unwittingly, sometimes maliciously, takes advantage of that "tough guy" spirit. Even requires it overtly and, more commonly, covertly.

Case Vignette:

I think about Billy. He lived with his two younger siblings and cared for them while his mother went out to "work" and get high. When she would come home after days away, she would be affectionate and appreciative of Billy, who, at five years old, learned to make peanut butter sandwiches so he and his two younger siblings could eat. This is an extreme case, and Billy developed psychosis and needed medication after Mom was arrested and the children went into Foster Care. Billy believed it was his responsibility to keep the family together.

Billy's wound is the **Tough Guy Mother Wound.**

Tough Guy Mother Wound is often associated with an Avoidant Attachment Style.

Big little Man Mother Wound – This Mother Wound occurs when a child is treated like an adult before their time, creating an **internal belief that if I have needs, I will disappoint others.**

BIG LITTLE MAN

What about the BIG LITTLE MAN? This child quickly learns that his role is to help others. The more he gives, the less he needs. The mother values her son's generosity, and over time he becomes a sounding board for her inner thoughts and worries. As he ages, he finds it harder and harder to know his own thoughts and feelings, fearing that if he has his own needs, he will disappoint others.

Case Vignette:

Let me tell you about Fred. He was a bright, energetic, and generous boy. Mom and Dad had what he describes as the perfect life. Two more siblings came after him, and he "gave" them his bedroom, wanting to help out. This simple, kind-hearted act was repeated and praised again and again.

Fast forward to his teen years, Mom wanted more out of her life and had an affair that ended the marriage, splitting the home in two.

The affair failed, and the marriage never recovered, even though she and Dad tried to reconcile.

Fred, having stayed at a job he hated for years until he got fired, struggles now to find meaning in his work or find another job.

Fred suffers from depression, as does his mother, which he thinks is another way to stay near her emotionally. Maybe so.

His Mother Wound has to do with a merging with his Mom, making it difficult for him to see his Mother Wound. He is very busy protecting Mom from having her feelings hurt, taking responsibility for her life, and thus avoiding his.

This mother wound is common in men. They become soldiers and warriors, especially if Dad is absent (or always working). They become the "man" of the house. Taking on more than they are ready for and are often valued for their sacrifice. I call this the **Big Little Man Mother Wound.**

One of the problems with this 'adorable' wound is that the little man thinks he is big and, as he grows, has a hard time with the frustrations of life and living. "I know what the best way to do it is, but no one listens to me" no one notices him in the way he expects to be noticed. He has a hard time believing he is valuable for who he is and often feels like the Big Little Man.

The **Big Little Man is often associated with the Anxious Attachment Style.**

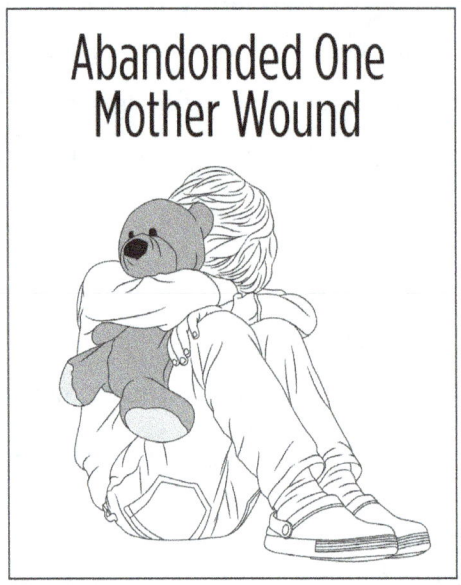

Abandoned One Mother Wound– is when mixed messages of praise and neglect create an internal belief that I don't matter, **I don't make sense, and I am ineffective.**

ABANDONED ONE

Much like the INVISIBLE MOTHER, the ABANDONED ONE is unfortunately common.

This child is told one thing and then shown something else. Mother's promises are broken, his ideas are overlooked or minimized, and he is teased or punished for having feelings and needs as a child.

ABANDONED ONE is a heart-wrenching wound and needs time and attention to heal.

Case Vignette:

Let's talk '**vulnerability.**' Take Nick. His mother always told him how much she loved him, but when she would take him out, it was with his Aunt or a friend, and he was ignored and expected to know what to do and how to act. Mother would later scold him for being so quiet and not being more involved. Nick was confused and hurt and had no one to share this with. He had an older sister, but she was the golden child, talented in music and academics. She had no interest in her younger brother from the day he was born and would side with her mother when Nick would be socially awkward.

Looking at Nick's history through his **Mother Wound**, you will see he was **given mixed messages** by being praised and then neglected and scorned, in addition to being set up to be in competition with his sister for not being like her.

Meanwhile, Nick enjoyed reading and playing "nerdy" electronic games alone in his room.

There was no place for Nick. His mother and father showed no interest in him, only in their own interests, which aligned with his sister.

Nick's wound is the **Abandoned One Mother Wound.**

The Abandoned One is often associated with a Disorganized Attachment Style.

F: Mother Wounds:

We just learned the six types of Mother Wounds found in men and women and their impact.

Pull out your journal, use the space below, or comment at the bottom of this lesson and follow these prompts:

I most identify with _____ Mother Wound(s) and I think my attachment style is _____

As I learn about my Mother Wound and my Attachment Style, the most supportive resource for me is _____
_____

I think about my parents and their parents and what type of Mother Wounds they have been exposed to.

Use your journal or the space below to write about what may have happened

_____
_____
_____
_____

In your journal or below use colors, lines, or cut-out pictures, create an image of what your Mother Wound looks and feels like now as an adult.

G: CONCLUSION & SUPPORT WORK

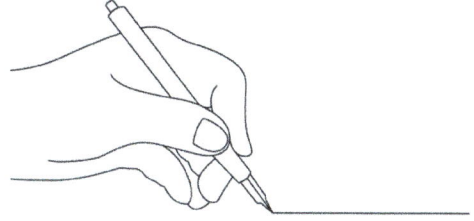

CONCLUSION:

We explored the types of Mother Wounds found in adults (men and women.)

We have also reflected on all the resources that we have gathered throughout the book to support us in our healing journey.

EXERCISE:

Think about which type of mother wound you have experienced.

Take your time, and see which, if any, resonates with you and your experience.

Let your thoughts, memories, and feelings surface, knowing and trusting; we are here to meet the wounded daughter or son with curiosity, compassion, and love.

Use the space below or in your journal to free-write

If there are wounded parts, let them know you are here, encouraging and supporting their healing process. In this way, bringing light to the shadows, you both may share.

Make a sketch – in words or images of what is coming up for you.

SUPPORT WORK:

Write or draw what comes up for you in your journal or art pad.

Make some notes. Try making these notes with your non-dominant hand. Trust what wants to come forth.

Please remember to find time to really feel the support of your resources and start making them a part of your life for the future, too, should you so choose.

Use Your Resources.

Review any of the meditations, "Best Self," "Calm Place," or "Mother Wound and Solar Plexus Exploration," and listen.

When you are done listening, I invite you to draw your feelings about it or journal.

Continue making Mandalas for what you want you want to keep in (inside the circle) and keep out (outside the circle)

Explore in your journal:

Is your self-talk changing?

Is it getting easier to ask for what you need and to let go of what you don't?

Support Stones

Make another Stone. Find that unpainted stone.

Take a look at your Tree of Strength.

Choose a word or two from the tree that calls you right now.

If that word was a color, what would it be?

Paint the stone that color, write or draw that word from your tree of strength onto your stone.

Continue to make "Support Stones." Keep them where you can access, see, rub, and feel them.

These are Resources for this workbook to help you.

Suggested Reading:

How is the book supporting you?

Have you finished reading it?

Did you find it helpful?

CHAPTER 9:
GIFT OF THE CRITICAL MOTHER

Overcoming the
Mother Wound

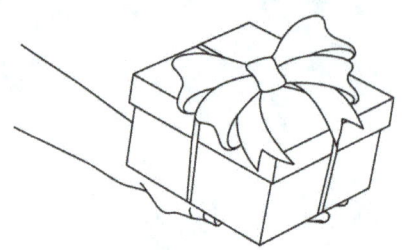

A: OVERVIEW & PRE-WORK

How are you doing?

How was the last lesson?

Are you ready for more?

This is our last blast before we wrap up.

This is a powerful exercise using art and writing.

Remember that you can always go back and listen to the earlier meditations and audio recordings and use any of the Resources you have learned.

FOR THIS LESSON YOU WILL NEED:

- You will need more time for this one. If possible, please give yourself an hour of quiet time.
- Your journal notes from Chapter 5.
- 12"x12" colored paper, glue sticks, a pen, and a black marker or sharpie.
- A dinner plate or compass.

SUPPORT EX1 ERCISES:

We will start with our Settling, Intention Setting, and Unscrambling exercises. To help you remember:

Settling Exercise ***APPENDIX L***

Setting an Intention Exercise ***APPENDIX M***

Unscrambling Exercise ***APPENDIX O***

Now that you are feeling settled, have your intention, and are unscrambled, let's go further.

Are you ready?

If so, let's go!

B: ART MAKING: MOSAIC "GIFT OF THE CRITICAL MOTHER" EXERCISE, originally in-visioned by Karla Hankes, PhD.

Before beginning this lesson listen to your Calm Place guided meditation.

Calm Place

This is a very powerful exercise, and I want you to get the most out of it. Below are the procedural steps to take:

Be sure to have your journal notes from the Dialogue with the Critic exercise from Chapter 5 for this exercise.

You will also need to have your 12" x 12" colored paper, glue sticks, pen, and a black marker or sharpie.

"You Are" Statements:

To begin, take your journal notes or the notes on the back of your drawing from Chapter 5B and, on a new page, convert each statement to start with "You are…"

For example, you would change "This picture is a mess" to "You are a mess." Or "I love this picture" would become "You are love."

Get my meaning? Your statements will likely be negative, which will help this exercise be more effective.

We don't want to avoid difficult feelings or overwhelm ourselves by experiencing a loop of negative thoughts and beliefs.

If this feels too icky, please take a break. Go to your Calm Place and have your Animal resource near you.

Once you are ready, here is the exercise:

Art Making:

Step 1: Layout all your 12"x12" colored paper so you can see them.

Step 2: Find a piece of colored paper (preferably pastel) that reminds you of your Best Self or your youngest, purest self with pure and innocent eyes and heart.

If you can't remember that part, think of someone dear to you, a child, a niece or nephew, or a neighbor. How do they feel? How do you feel about them? Allow yourself to recall any tender moments.

Example

Step 3: Take your Compass or dinner- plate and make a black circle on the colored piece of 12"x12" paper you chose.

Example

RESOURCE - Check in with your Calm Place, just for a moment.

Step 4: Turn that colored paper over (so you do not see the black circle), and on the back, write a 10-minute stream of consciousness of how this little one feels or felt. In her purest, most innocent, heart-opened space, she existed.

Example

No judgment: she does not know that it exists.

Imagine how that innocent one feels.

On this side of the paper, write positive words or phrases, even images, to describe how this child feels, how this child responds to this color, and what it brings up for the child (joy, peace, toys, pets, etc.).

Once your pen meets the paper, do not lift it up. Have fun, and make sure to **fill up that page** staying connected with that innocent one. Take around 10 minutes with this

MAY THIS BOOK BRING HOPE AND INSPIRATION

Write as if you are that joyous, happy, and innocent child.

The little one that popped out of mommy's belly. The one that came into life open-hearted, curious, and loving. Fill up the page, feel your words, and embody that young, pure Self.

Example

RESOURCE – Check in with your animal and make that connection momentarily.

Step 5: Get the negative notes you have from earlier lessons, especially Module 5B (Dialogue with the Critic).

Step 6: Turn the paper over to see only the black circle.

Example

Pick up that paper and read about 5-10 negative comments out loud, if possible.

Each time you read a negative statement, tear your paper completely from one side to the other.

You don't need to write it down. Simply read it out loud, rip your paper from side to side after you read a negative comment, and then lay the torn pieces to the side for now.

Step 7: Look at your unused colored paper again. Let yourself be drawn to a color (preferably a pure, saturated color) that makes you feel better. Feel it, try not to think about it, then choose it.

Step 8: With glue sticks, **paste the side of the new torn paper with writing on it down** (so you can't see the words but are guided by the lines of the black circle) onto the new jewel-colored paper.

Leave a little space between the pieces so the new color can show through, and use the black line to help guide your placement.

Example

Look at what is there now.

Notice how it makes you feel.

See what that little one has gone through.

Can you see the beauty of your image?

The complexity?

The individuality?

As in Leonard Cohen's "Anthem," he famously wrote, "There is a crack in everything; that's how the light gets in."

Similar to the Japanese pottery tradition of "Kintsugi" we are putting the broken pieces back together and embracing the imperfections, as we create a unique and beautiful piece of art.

Journal Prompts to Take this Deeper:

Bring out your journal. Write what you are feeling now and what you experienced during this exercise.

What did it bring up for you? Either when making it, looking at it, or how it is making you feel right now.

Feel free to upload your mosaics to the Facebook Group to find like-minded folk. I pop in there too!

That was not an easy exercise!

Congratulations on doing this healing and thank your little one too!

Share on the OCMW Facebook page if you are up for it.

The next lesson is our last - I look forward to you being there!

C: CONCLUSION & SUPPORT WORK

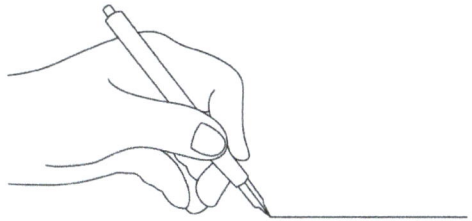

CONCLUSION:

As the final art-making experience, you created a Mosaic to show that your experiences are what make you unique. In this way, you learned about your gift from your critical mother.

Your homework is similar to the last two modules' because I hope you implement and make the resources part of your life. The more you use them, the more support they will offer you.

What's calling you?

I've been providing resources throughout this course to help you have tools for your life to help.

The goal of this workbook is to incorporate these resources into your life.

Now, I will challenge you to notice what you need and choose the resource you are most drawn to.

You may feel like one is enough, or you may need 10. There's no right or wrong here.

As a reminder, here is a list of resources that we've covered:

Settling, Intention Setting, and Unscrambling Exercises

Tree of Strength

Support Stones

Guided Resource Meditation "Your Best Self."

Guided Resource Meditation "Calm Place" + Drawing.

Mandalas: "What you Need," "What to Keep," "Contain the Critic "Animal Mandala" "What is in my control?", Solar Plexus "Mother Wound."

Guided Resource Meditation, "Your Animal" + Drawing

Guided Resource Meditation, "Exploring the Mother Wound"

Gift of the Critical Mother Mosaic

Explore in your journal or below:

What did you feel drawn to in this module for resources, and how did it help?

Finishing Your Supplemental Book:

If you've finished, what are your overall thoughts on your book?

You can also look back at your insights in your journal to see how this book has impacted your life, and comment below or in your journal.

EPILOGUE

Overcoming the Mother Wound

I am grateful for the physical support, education, and health my parents gave me that has enabled me to live a productive life.

I am also grateful for my childhood and the pain that ensued, providing a grist for developing healing programs I want to share with the world.

A: OVERVIEW & POST-WORK

You did it! You made it to Lesson 10. Let's take a moment to celebrate your hard work.

It's not easy to explore these feelings, but seeing your progress is worthwhile.

Our final chapter is about pulling it all together and seeing how far you have come.

Don't worry; there's no judgment or right or wrong way to take this course.

FOR OUR CLOSING ACTIVITY YOU WILL NEED:

- Your past art-making exercises.
- Your journal from the entire course.
- Two different colored crayons or markers.
- Time to take the Post-Course Questionnaire and create a new Mother-Daughter drawing.

SUPPORT EXERCISES:

We will start with our Settling, Intention Setting, and Unscrambling exercises. To help you remember:

Settling Exercise ***APPENDIX L***

Setting an Intention Exercise ***APPENDIX M***

Unscrambling Exercise ***APPENDIX O***

Are you doing these beginning exercises on your own? Do you find them helpful?

So curious! I'm open to any feedback, as usual.

B: PUTTING IT ALL TOGETHER

Take a look at all the art and writing you have made during this course.

Here are some of the amazing resources you now have handy:

Your Journal

Settling, Intention Setting, and Unscrambling Exercises

Tree of Strength

Support Stones

Guided Resource Meditation "Your Best Self".

Guided Resource Meditation "Calm Place" + Drawing.

Mandalas: "What you Need", "What to Keep", "Contain the Critic "Animal Mandala" "What is in my control?",Solar Plexus "Mother Wound."

Guided Resource Meditation, "Your Animal" + Drawing

Guided Resource Meditation, "Exploring the Mother Wound"

Gift of the Critical Mother Mosaic

C: POST-COURSE QUESTIONNAIRE

Take your **Post-Course Assessment**

Bear in mind that the post-course assessment contains the same questions as the pre-course assessment - this is a tool to assist you in comparing how you felt at both stages of the course - start and finish - and what changes occurred.

Self-Assessment Questionnaire

This self-assessment questionnaire should be done at the beginning of the course and again upon completion as a valuable tool to track your progress and identify where you may want future support.

Questions are written in the first person, please answer to the best of your ability:

1. When I wake up in the morning

    a. It is the best time of the day so let me stretch, move, look around, I'm glad to wake up.

    b. I think about all the stuff I have to do and can't stay in bed, so I get up.

    c. I'm annoyed that I have to get up, but I just want to stay in bed and not be bothered.

2. When I go to bed at night

    a. I fall asleep easily and usually sleep straight till it's time to get up.

    b. I toss and turn, thinking about the day, wondering about tomorrow.

    c. It doesn't matter if I fall asleep early or late, I wake up through the night and often have disturbing dreams.

3. When I look at myself in the mirror

    a. I see a beautiful soul that has done a great job with her life so far.

    b. I see someone that needs to do a lot of work but might be okay someday.

    c. I see someone that needs help and I wish I knew how to help myself better.

4. My friendships

a. I have a few close friends, especially 1 or 2 who I confide in deeply.

b. I like people, but I keep meeting people who are demanding and critical.

c. It is hard for me to get close to other people, I don't think they like me.

5. My romantic relations

    a. I am in a long-term serious relationship where I feel accepted and supported.

    b. I am in an "on again off again" passionate relationship, which is usually my pattern.

    c. I usually get involved with someone who is not available or abusive.

6. When I have time to myself

    a. I like to take time to recharge with a creative endeavor or spend time in nature.

    b. I like to be busy, retail therapy usually does the trick.

    c. I just zone out and get kind of lost, not sure what to do. Then I start to berate myself for not using my time better.

7. When I meet someone new

    a. I am curious to find out who they are and for them to know who I am.

    b. I prefer to let them reach out if they want to get to know me.

    c. New people make me nervous, I don't think they'll like me anyway.

8. If I need to make an important decision

    a. I sit quietly, view the situation, and ask for inner guidance.

    b. I write down all the pros and cons methodically and see what makes sense.

    c. I ask other people what I should do after exhausting the above options. Tally your results to keep for the end of the course.

Add how many you put for each:

a's b's e's

Compare this assessment with the one you took at the start of this book

Mother-Child Drawing Prompt

Gather art materials of your choice, which may or may not be from the list provided in the Appendix. Find a comfortable place where you will not be disturbed for 10 to 20 minutes.

Settle in your space, take a deep breath in, hold it for a moment, and then let it slowly as if you are blowing through a straw. I suggest doing that at least one more time to activate your rest and digest or parasympathetic nervous system.

Then, think of a time in your past, go back as far as you'd like, and see what image comes up of you and your mother.

Draw this picture of you and your mother.

Add the date and title of the drawing.

Compare this drawing with the one you made at the start of this book.

D: MOTHER-CHILD DIALOGUE ART-MAKING AND JOURNALING EXERCISE.

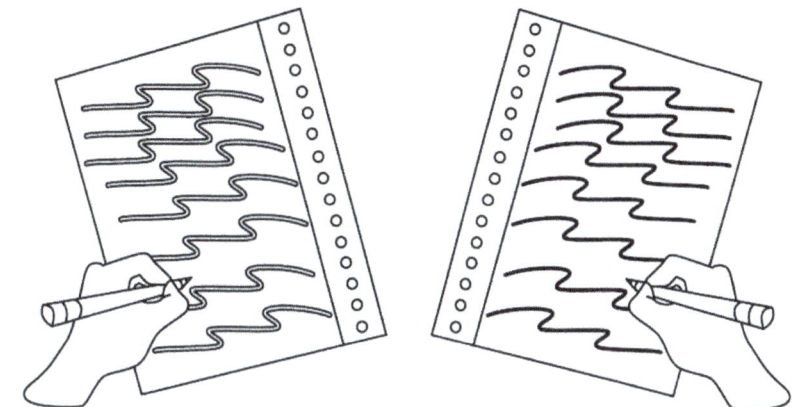

Look at the picture you just made of you and your mother. What do you notice?

We are going to have a conversation between you and your mother in the picture.

In your right hand, be the voice of your mother in your picture (choose a color); in your left hand, be that small child (choose a different color).

What does that child REALLY want to say?

Be sure the child has their Animal near and is well-rested from spending time in their Calm Place.

Take 10-20 minutes to have a new dialogue. Mom in right hand, little one in left.

Afterward, ask yourself these questions:

Does it feel different?

Does it feel complete?

Look at the colors of the words:

Is one color more dominant than the other?

How does this make you feel?

Take time for reflection on these assessments.

I bet you've come a long way, and I hope you've adopted many of the resources and will keep using them.

POST-SCRIPT

You can share your experiences with this workbook with a trusted friend, a curious pet, your therapist (if you are working with one), or your coach, healer, etc.

You can also reach out to me directly: **mari@creativehealngintegration.com**

We have covered a lot of material in these lessons. I hope this has given you a better, or an expanded sense of, your relationship with your mother and how this impacts you now.

If you'd like more support or take the course online with me in my Overcoming the Mother Wound Program here is a direct link to sign up: https://www.creativehealingintegration.com/evergreen-self-study-course1.

You can also check out my offerings on my website and sign up for the Creative Healing Integration (CHI) mailing list to be notified of new programs, courses, and guided meditations: www.creativehealingintegration.com

Thank you. I am deeply grateful to you for taking the time to meet and interact with your Mother Wound to help support your healing journey, wherever that may be for you today.

A journey close to my heart and true to my approach to healing.

Warmly,

ACKNOWLEDGEMENTS

IV

Overcoming the
Mother Wound

This book is inspired by the online course of the same name, which is the culmination of many years of researching, learning about, and working with attachment disorders, developmental trauma, theories, and techniques for healing. As you may discover, Mind/Body, Art/Psyche approaches heavily influence how I teach and help others heal.

In many ways, the OCMW workbook and course are original; however, it would not have existed without learning what I've learned. In this way, I have borrowed or been inspired by others, edited it, and made it my owm; whenever I know I am borrowing, I will reference the source.

Here I'd like to acknowledge my teachers, healers, and divine guidance in creating this course.

I'd like to thank my clients, colleagues, and virtual assistants who knowingly and unknowingly helped and inspired me along the way.

I'd also like to apologize for any oversight if I have not referenced you directly.

Warmly,

APPENDIX A

Art Materials List

11x17" paper

12x 12 multi-color paper

Blank paper large enough for a dinner size plate

Colored Crayons

Colored Pencils

Compass or dinner size plate for circle

Cray-pas

Glue Sticks

Journal for Writing

Markers

Paintbrush (s)

Pen (s)

Sketching Pencil

Sharpie or black marker

Stones (rocks)

Water-based paints

Your favorite drawing materials

APPENDIX B

Book Recommendations

Here are a few suggested books you might find interesting to supplement your learning. You may purchase them here: https://www.creativehealingintegration.com/evergreen-books or elsewhere, or even get them from your public library.

Adult Children of Emotionally Immature Parents, Lindsay Gibson

Written by a clinical psychologist this book unveils the effects of being parented by parents that needed parenting. The book looks at what happened to the child, and how the adult child can heal from the pain, neglect, and confusion of this experience.

Daughter Detox, Peg Streep

This author unpacks her research about daughters who have been harmed in their relationship with their mothers. The book is structured is a self-help format but has many useful information and strategies on ways to heal.

Discovering the Inner Mother, Bethany Webster

This powerful self-help book supports female empowerment and growth. Written in 2020 the author points out that everyone has a mother wound, and shares ideas of how to work with it.

I Don't Want to Talk About It, Terry Real

The author explores male depression using case vignettes and personal experiences. The book does not stop there and shows us ways to use our pain to heal, grow, and restore relationships.

Mother Hunger, Kelly McDaniel

The intention of this book is to help women break the cycle of negative patterns of behavior. While offering plenty of case vignettes, tools, and psychoeducation the author traces the cycle back to the earliest relationship, the mother. The book includes self-help exercises of support.

My Mother My Self, Nancy Friday

This classic, research-based book was first published in the 1970s. Nancy Friday focuses on the unique & important relationship between a mother and daughter and hints at the concept of intergenerational transmission of trauma.

Necessary Losses, Judith Viorst

This book addresses grief. According to the author we must grieve in order to gain a truer sense of who we are in the world. Grieving includes loss of our mother's protection, our younger selves, and some of our dreams.

Real Boys, William Pollack

This book, steeped in groundbreaking research, challenges our assumed notions of boys and manhood. The author lets us know how easy it is for boys to slip through the cracks and encourages parents to reevaluate what real boys need and understand the Boy Code.

Reviving Ophelia, Pipher and Gilliam

This book contains insightful research and real-world examples of the challenges young women face and ways to address them. This is an updated version of the original 1994 version reframing what the author calls "girl poisoning culture." The revised edition is updated by the author, who was a teenager at the time of the original publication

The Drama of the Gifted Child, Alice Miller

This book, first published in 1997, looks at causes, types, and preventions of childhood trauma. The Gift, of course, is surviving the abuse

APPENDIX C

GUIDED MEDITATION

Animal Resource Meditation

I recommend you record this guided meditation to have it handy and listen to it whenever you'd like. Or can have someone you love to record it for you.

Give yourself 10 – 20 minutes to settle, listen, and respond in writing or art-making about what you see, feel, or whatever else you experienced.

When you are ready, find yourself in a quiet spot where you will not be interrupted or disturbed to listen to this brief and gentle guided meditation and see what animal is revealed to you:

When you see the word "pause," do not say the word out loud but be still and "pause" in silence.

About your animal resource:

This is not an animal you know or that you've seen. It has no name.

Here is your ANIMAL MEDITATION RESOURCE:

Find a comfortable place to be and sit in a comfortable spot.

A place where you can feel the support of the ground or floor beneath you, where your back is supported, and you are comfortable.

Begin to notice your breathing…., in…, out, breathing in and breathing out, noticing if the breath is fast, slow, that's it, allow the breath to come into your chest, into your belly, and then release and let go.

Feel the rhythm of your breathing, breathing deeper and deeper, as you feel the support beneath you, the space around you, letting sounds filter through you, letting any sensations come and go.

Letting any thoughts come and go.

As the body relaxes, the noises in the brain can get louder; that's what the brain does, allow them to come and go, let the noise come and go, turning down the dial just for a few moments, that's it, keeping the volume low, paying attention to your breathing, pause.

And when you feel even more comfortable, I want you to bring up an ANIMAL.

This is not an animal you have ANY relation with or have seen somewhere and know it by name.

Let this animal come to you; let it appear.

There is no right or wrong animal; see what is there and what wants to come forth.

When your animal has arrived, look into its eyes and let it look into yours, *pause.*

Tilt your forehead towards each other, looking into each other's eyes, *pause.*

Does your animal have a scent? Is your animal making any sounds?

Standing with your animal, reach out and touch the surface of your animal and feel its texture.

pause.

Gently put your hand over your animal's heart, feel the heart beating, and allow your animal to put a hand over your heart.

Feel each other's hearts beating, *pause.*

Let your animal know you see it, that you feel it, p*ause.*

Let your animal know you know it is there, and the animal let you know it is here for you.

pause.

We're coming back now.

Slowly begin to breathe a little deeper, become aware of your belly rising, your chest rising, the sensation of breath coming in and out.

Become aware of the ground beneath you, the surface supporting you; start wiggling your fingers, toes, wrists, and ankles; begin to stretch and move your body, fluttering your eyes open.

Look around the room, noticing what is in your environment.

Rub your palms on your thighs. Come back, come back, you're back.

Drink a glass of water, make sure you are awake and alert!

APPENDIX D

GUIDED MEDITATION

Best Self

Please read and record the following guided meditation, then play it back as you relax and listen:

When you see the word "pause," do not say the word out loud but be still and "pause" in silence.

Start by making yourself comfortable, lying down or sitting.

Begin to notice your breath, inhaling to the count of 3 and exhaling to the count of 6; continue inhaling and exhaling, spending a little more time on the exhalation.

Soften or close your eyes as you listen to these words:

Think of a time, a moment, when you felt like your true self, *pause.*

However far back or far you need to go, see what comes to you, *pause.*

What was that like?

Is it something you experienced?

Something you completed, accomplished and felt good about.

Did you dream about it?

Take a moment and scan over your life; what pops up?

How did it make you feel?

Whether anyone noticed or not, you knew how good you felt. Feel that feeling, *pause.*

Notice how your body feels, *pause.*

What do your eyes see? *pause.*

How do you stand? pause, what is your energy like?

This is your BEST SELF. Take a moment and look at your best self.

What do you see? Stand next to your Best Self. How does it feel to be with your Best Self?

Take a moment and take in what it is like to be with your best self.

Remember these important feelings and characteristics.

APPENDIX E

GUIDED MEDITATION

Calm Place

Below is a Meditation that can help you feel calm by creating a special place for yourself.

This place is created in your imagination, and you can access it and feel it anytime you want.

Recommendation: record the words below and then play the audio when you are in a place where you can close your eyes and listen.

When you see the word "pause," do not say the word out loud but be still and "pause" in silence.

Give yourself 10 – 20 minutes to settle, listen, and respond in writing or art-making about what you see, feel, or whatever else you experienced.

To start, find a spot where you won't be disturbed for at least 10 minutes, longer if you'd like to have time to settle before and time to reflect and even draw your experience afterward.

You can imagine this as you read, but I highly recommend recording the meditation on a device such as your phone so that it can be handy later, too. Also, we will be using this meditation throughout this book, and this way, you'll be able to come back to your calm place whenever you'd like.

Make yourself as comfortable as possible, but not so comfortable that you will fall asleep. If you do fall asleep, trust that you will still hear exactly what it is you need to hear.

When we listen to guided meditations, it is best to let go of our thinking brain and trust the unconscious is attentively listening. This way, our mind can take a break and let other, less active, but equally valuable parts of us be in charge.

Let's begin:

Start to become more aware of your breathing, noticing the rhythm, pace, and sound of the breath.

On your next inhale, hold for a moment, then release slowly and fully.

Again, breathing in, holding, and letting go.

Continue breathing, letting the body do all the work. Letting thoughts come and go, noticing, and being.

As you begin to relax, think of a place, real or imagined, where you feel most comfortable, most at ease, most at peace.

This may be a place you've read about, seen in a movie, dreamed about or even been to.

Take your time and see what comes to you, *pause*.

Have you found it? *pause*.

Look around; what is there? *pause*.

What colors? *pause*.

What feelings go with this place? *pause*.

Are you outside? Are you in nature? p*ause*.

Are you inside? What are there furnishings? *pause*.

What sounds do you hear? *pause*.

What time of day is it? *pause*.

What temperature? *pause*.

Is there a breeze? *pause*.

What do you smell? *pause*.

Take note and hang out in your calm place for a few moments.

APPENDIX F

Mother Wound Solar Plexus Meditation

Start by making yourself comfortable, lying down, or sitting up.

Ensure you won't be disturbed for 10-20 minutes.

Have your journal and/or drawing materials nearby for the exercise portion of today's lesson.

REMINDER: *Throughout the book, I reference boys/girls, daughters/sons, and he/she interchangeably as we refer to the mother wound.*

When you are ready, read and record this brief meditative transmission, then relax and listen to it:

When you see the word "pause," do not say the word out loud but be still and "pause" in silence.

We all have chakras, energy centers in our bodies, and we are going to focus on the solar chakra just above your belly button.

Start by sitting upright or lying on your back.

Close your eyes, and take a deep breath in, and inhale through the entire center of your body, especially your belly.

Hold the breath there for just a moment, then focus your energy around your navel, *pause,* and slowly exhale, allowing your belly button to sink towards your spine as you let your breath out.

We are connecting to our energy center, our life force, the area that holds the memory of the cord that connected us in our mother's womb, *pause.*

Our life growing inside of her. Our body living in hers. Here is the Solar Plexus Chakra, associated with our sense of self, our sense of aliveness and identity, and connected to our experiences with our mothers.

The mother wound is a trauma handed down from mother to child, *pause.*

Often, the mother has experienced her own disillusionments and traumas and unconsciously carries her experiences of loss, rage, neglect, abuse, unfulfilled dreams, and grief deep in their psyche.

Passing down through the generations unresolved pain and sorrow to future generations, *pause*.

Notice what is coming up for you.

Take note of your thoughts, feelings, and bodily sensations.

Then begin to breath deeper and deeper, becoming aware of the weight of your body, start wiggling your toes and your fingers, flutter your eyes open.

Stretch if you need to, and grab a glass of water. You may be moving some energy as you feel and experience things related to your mother wound.

No worries, this is only energy, and it just wants to move. A natural, healthy response when we are learning and growing

APPENDIX G

Types of Mother Wounds Guided Meditation

Below is the written meditation, please read and record it and listen when you are in a place where you will not be disturbed for at least 15 minutes:

When you see the word pause do not read the word out loud but be still and "pause" in silence.

Please allow yourself to take in only what you need for today, knowing you can come back at any time to listen and receive what you need when you need it.

In case we have not had an ideal or rather a good enough, early relationship with our early caretakers, we develop wounds.

Attachment theorists refer to wounds by styles such as avoidant, ambivalent, and disorganized.

After listening to these types of wounds, you can sense into which ones resonate with you. It's not uncommon to have more than one experience with our early caretakers. Let's go a little deeper into the mother wound.

The thing about this wound is we can't see it or touch it with our hands, and yet it is there. It is here. Each wound is unique, as each child is unique, as each mother-child relationship is unique.

So, let's slow down. Give this some time, some space. If you need to take a break at any time, please do.

This guided meditation is not meant to overwhelm you, and if that is happening, please pause or bring one of your resources with you.

If you're still here, let's begin.

Start by noticing the surface you're sitting on.

Noticing how your feet are meeting the ground.

Notice your breath.

Allow any sounds or smells around you to be there, giving space to whatever needs to be there.

Coming all the way inside, following your breath as you inhale, sensing your throat, chest, stomach, belly, and as you exhale, allowing your hips to soften and spread. Feeling the weight of your legs and feet.

Breathing in and breathing out. Breathing in and breathing out.

Now, recalling our meditation with your belly, your navel chakra, just above your belly button, take a deep inhale, hold the breath there for just a moment, feeling the energy in your navel, and exhale.

Slowly dropping your navel toward your spine as you release your breath.

We are connecting with your navel energy, the center of your life force.

The memory of the cord in the womb that connected us to our mothers.

The cord that's been physically disconnected a long time ago, yet the connection lingers.

The navel center is associated with our sense of self, with our deepest sense of aliveness and security. Self, with a capital S.

The mother connection is handed down from mother to child, generation to generation.

What is your connection? *pause*

Is there love? *pause*

Hurt? *pause*

Rage? *pause*

All that and more? Less?

Many children and many adults have many different experiences with this connection. And all children and adults have this connection. What is yours? *pause*

No matter your mother's intention, what was your experience with your mother?

Here are six primary wounds a mother can pass down to a boy or girl child.

Critical mother. The critical mother wound. Was she the critical mother? No matter what you did or do for this mother it is never enough or it is too much. You are too loud or too quiet, too sensitive or too strong.

You're either too much or not enough. She attacks you for being you. This message teaches you to hate herself, and with an internal belief I am defective.

This child loses their voice and their joy in order to survive. They learn It is not safe to be themselves.

The critical mother can be physically and or verbally cruel. She may craftily manipulate you with her words or outright yell and beat you. Her tone may be maternal but her message is sharp and cold.

Giving you the pain of her own hidden wounds of loss, regret, and hopelessness that she is unable to accept and own.

The child of the critical mother may live with fear and anger towards themselves and others.

Living in a negative loop unbeknownst to themselves.

The next wound is the Invisible mother.

When there is an **Invisible** mother, the child is left to their own resources and learns to fend for themselves. Turning inward to their inner world, hoping to meet their own needs in relationships where others could not.

The invisible mother births an unmothered child.

This mother may be ill, deceased or not physically present and not available to her child's needs.

If withholding of love and attention towards her child is intentional, as in the critical mother, the child experiences emotional abuse.

The child gets the message, I'm not important, I don't matter, no one can see me. When the child absorbs and believes this message, anxiety, depression, and other self-destructive or addictive behaviors develop over time.

A physically present but emotionally absent mother incurs a wound on the child. This is another form of the invisible mother wound.

Imagine a well-intending mother attending to her child's basic needs but unable to connect with the child's emotional needs. Here, the mother wound is indirect, most likely due to the child's mother's mother wound and their lack of attunement. This is a wound to the psyche, not easy to see, confusing, and painful.

The pain is even greater if the child witnesses the mother making an emotional connection with another sibling, close relatives or friends.

When a mother wound is fuzzy and unclear, it is not as quick to identify.

This wound takes patience, tenderness, and time to heal.

Even if the mother tries her best, it is a wound.

Next, the **Engulfing** mother wound. An engulfing mother may be physically overwhelming toward her child, ignoring or intruding on her personal space and in some way keeping her from experiencing the world in her own way.

The engulfing mother confuses her needs with her child's Burdening her child with her own needs, the child of an engulfing mother finds it hard to feel who they are, what they want, believe, or need. Especially if their needs are other than their mother's expectations of them.

The child learns to believe they are supposed to take care of their mother's needs instead of their mother taking care of theirs. An engulfing mother that is also critical, verbally or physically abusive can be toxic.

This child will usually either merge and stay near mother or move far away in adulthood in an attempt to feel separate and free.

It is hard for this child to simply be and develop into who that are on the inside. They often feel trapped so if they leave it's as if they escape, physically, from their mother. Without working through their wound they can be very controlling about their space, feelings, and time.

Now let's look at the **Big Little Man.** This child quickly learns that their role is to help others.

The more they give, the less they need.

The mother values her child's generosity, and over time, they become a sounding board for her inner thoughts and worries.

As the child ages, they find it harder and harder to know their own thoughts and feelings, fearing if they have their own needs, they will disappoint others.

Then we have the **Tough Guy.** The TOUGH GUY is similar to the BIG LITTLE MAN, but feel the difference between those types of wounds.

Social norms, traditions, and expectations treat boys differently than girls. Girls are generally considered more fragile, sensitive, and needy. Boys are thought to be rough, tough, loud, and dirty. Boys don't cry; boys are strong. To be vulnerable is to be a sissy.

We know **so** much more now, but cultures and even our unconscious biases may not have caught up.

The Tough Guy mother wound touches the heart of the masculine and is also seen in women.

Their genuine, generous heart that steps up when there is a need.

Here, the mother unwittingly, sometimes maliciously, takes advantage of that "tough guy" spirit.

Even requires it overtly and, more commonly, covertly.

This child learns that their role is to take care of others, override their own needs, physical and emotional, and be there for mom, the family, and others with little regard for themselves.

Not to be forgotten is the **Abandoned One** Mother Wound.

This wound grows out of the child being given mixed messages.

Being promised one thing and being given another thing or nothing at all.

Or being showered with attention in public and then ignored in private, or vice versa, creating an internal belief that **I am dispensable, I don't matter, I don't make sense, and I am ineffective**.

Pause

So, let's just take a little time to take in this information and see what resonates, see what makes sense, what feels afar, what feels close, and just let it all sift in and sift out.

Pause

Take in what you want from this experience and leave whatever you want to leave behind, behind.

Pause

We are going to be slowly coming back out of this guided meditation.

Pause

Become aware of your body being supported and becoming aware of your breathing.

Become aware of any sounds around your space.

Become aware of the temperature of the space you are in.

Feel the weight of your body.

Become aware of your breathing.

Flutter your eyes open, look around the room you are in.

Bring your hands together as if in prayer, and rub them together very quickly, stimulating the nerve in your fingers, and helping you become even more and more alert.

Take a couple of sips of air, drink some water, tap your shoulders, tap your chest, tap the top of your head, and really make sure you are back.

APPENDIX H

Mother-Child Drawing Prompt:

Gather art materials of your choice, which may or may not be from the list provided in the Appendix.

Find a comfortable place where you will not be disturbed for 10 to 20 minutes.

Settle in your space, take a deep breath in, hold it for a moment, and then let it slowly as if you are blowing through a straw. I suggest doing that at least once more to activate your rest and digest or parasympathetic nervous system.

Then, think of a time in your past, go back as far as you'd like, and see what image comes up of you and your mother.

Draw this picture of you and your mother.

Add the date and title of the drawing.

Set the drawing aside for now.

APPENDIX I

Mother Wound Self-Assessment:

This self-assessment questionnaire should be done at the beginning of the course and again upon completion as a valuable tool to track your progress and identify where you may want future support.

Questions are written in the first person, please answer to the best of your ability:

1. When I wake up in the morning

    a. It is the best time of the day so let me stretch, move, look around, I'm glad to wake up.

    b. I think about all the stuff I have to do and can't stay in bed, so I get up.

    c. I'm annoyed that I have to get up, but I just want to stay in bed and not be bothered.

2. When I go to bed at night

    a. I fall asleep easily and usually sleep straight till it's time to get up.

    b. I toss and turn, thinking about the day, wondering about tomorrow.

    c. It doesn't matter if I fall asleep early or late, I wake up through the night and often havedisturbing dreams.

3. When I look at myself in the mirror

    a. I see a beautiful soul that has done a great job with her life so far.

    b. I see someone that needs to do a lot of work but might be okay someday.

    c. I see someone that needs help and I wish I knew how to help myself better.

4. My friendships

    a. I have a few close friends, especially 1 or 2 who I confide in deeply.

    b. I like people, but I keep meeting people who are demanding and critical.

    c. It is hard for me to get close to other people, I don't think they like me.

5. My romantic relations

    a. I am in a long-term serious relationship where I feel accepted and supported.

    b. I am in an "on again off again" passionate relationship, which is usually my pattern.

    c. I usually get involved with someone who is not available or abusive.

6. When I have time to myself

    a. I like to take time to recharge with a creative endeavor or spend time in nature.

    b. I like to be busy, retail therapy usually does the trick.

    c. I just zone out and get kind of lost, not sure what to do. Then I start to berate myself for not using my time better.

7. When I meet someone new

    a. I am curious to find out who they are and for them to know who I am.

    b. I prefer to let them reach out if they want to get to know me.

    c. New people make me nervous, I don't think they'll like me anyway.

8. If I need to make an important decision

    a. I sit quietly, view the situation, and ask for inner guidance.

    b. I write down all the pros and cons methodically and see what makes sense.

    c. I ask other people what I should do after exhausting the above options. Tally your results to keep for the end of the course.

Add how many you put for each:

a's b's e's

Compare this assessment with the one you took at the start of this book

APPENDIX J

Overcoming the Mother Wound (OCMW) course links

Creative Healing Integration Website:

https://www.creativehealingintegration.com/

Evergreen Overcoming the Mother Wound Course Bundle:

https://www.creativehealingintegration.com/evergreen-self-study-course1

Overcoming the Mother Wound Program:

https://www.creativehealingintegration.com/overcoming-the-mother-wound

APPENDIX K

Self Care Sheet

Keep a journal dedicated to the book. Here, you can write or draw what happened for you and what didn't happen. What you want, don't want, what you liked, and how you felt, thought, or anything else that comes up for you as you work on Overcoming the Mother Wound.

Get used to spending time with your thoughts and feelings in a supportive, curious way.

Do 1 kind thing for yourself a day – This could be acknowledging your bravery for being interested in this book, appreciating how good you are at keeping your word, getting rest, eating healthy, or noticing being kind to yourself or someone else.

Take time to breathe – Take about 2 minutes in the morning and 2 minutes at the end of the day to focus on your breath. Use an exercise we've practiced in the book, like the Square Breath (breathing in for the count of 4, pausing for the count of 4, exhaling to the count of 4, and pausing to the count of 4 before repeating that for 4 more rounds). Sometimes, just paying attention to your breathing for 2 minutes is all you need.

APPENDIX L

Settling Exercise

Find a comfortable place where you won't be disturbed.

Sit comfortably. Feel your feet meeting the ground and sense any support to your body. Is the support beneath you? Behind you?

Start noticing your breath. See if you can count how long you inhale and how long you exhale.

Sometimes, just noticing your breath is settling.

Some people find it helpful to breathe in for the count of 4, pause for the count of 4, exhale to the count of 4, and pause to the count of 4 before repeating that for 4 more rounds. It is also called the "square breath."

APPENDIX M

Setting an Intention

Stand and feel your feet on the ground. Bounce a little up and down to feel the weight of your body. As you breath feel your breath all the way into your belly, and exhale fully.

Perhaps counting how long you inhale and then doubling that count as you exhale. Do that about 3 times.

If this makes you dizzy, perhaps breathe for fewer counts. 3 in and 6 out is usually a comfortable count.

Take a moment to feel in for what it is you need today, what you'd like to take in from today's lesson, and what you'd like to bring to today's lesson.

Let an Intention for today come to mind. Accept whatever comes.

Now, stand with your legs a little further than your shoulders, in a "horse stance" as if riding a horse as if your feet are in stirrups, feet point straight forward, feet flat on the ground.

Bounce, bending your knees gently, and feel the ground beneath you.

Start with hands on top of heart, the left hand on top of the right for women, right hand on top of left for men(a qigong tradition but you can do whatever is comfortable), hold there for a moment, set an intention for your lesson.

Inhale expand that intention out as your reach your arms out, opening your heart space, stretching your arms wide, and opening your intention to the world.

Exhale, pull in and receive what you need (hug in) to support this intention, wrap yourself in an embrace.

Repeat this for a total of 3 x.

Open your intention from your heart and hug in and receive what you need.

APPENDIX N

Tree of Strength

The Tree of Strength is a great support for building on neuroplasticity. This exercise helps remind us of things about ourselves we either forgot, did not realize, or valued.

Directions and an example are below, for your reference.

Grab your 11" x 17" paper, pencils, pens, and markers.

Lay one hand on the paper, and your fingers spread with part of your arm on the paper.

Trace your arm and hand, leaving the tips of the **finger's tips open.**

Lift arm.

At the end of the open fingertips, extend the drawing to create more branches.

Draw several leaves at the end of the "branches," making them large enough to **write in each one.**

On each leaf, write one thing that helps you get through a difficult time – personal strengths, coping strategies, enjoyable activities, supportive people, etc.

Create as many leaves as you want, but no less than 5.

When finished:

Look at your Tree of Strength; be with it for a few moments, and notice what it is like to see your strengths.

MAY THIS BOOK BRING HOPE AND INSPIRATION

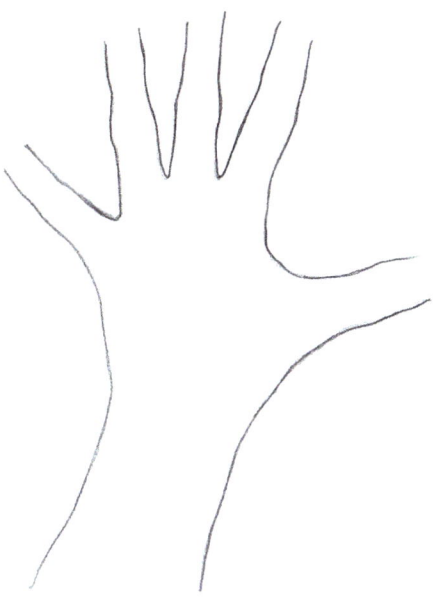

(STEP 1)

(STEP 2)

APPENDIX O

Unscramble Exercise

This simple pose helps to bring all your meridian energy into alignment (meridians are the energetic 'highways' of the body).

If you're feeling scrambled, confused, or stressed, this can bring you right back to your center!

This is also a pose that many children do intuitively.

Breathe in through the nose and out through the mouth.

Stand with feet side by side.

Cross one foot over the other and stand like that.

Extend your arms out in front of you, thumbs pointing down with palms facing away.

Cross one arm over the other, bring the hands together, and interlace your fingers. Then scoop them up and under.

Your legs are crossed, and your arms are crossed.

Breathe in through the nose and out through the mouth. Repeat 3 times.

Then reverse it. Switch hands: Unhook your hands, cross the other one on top, and hook them up.

Then uncross your feet and cross the other one on top.

Breathe in through the nose and out through the mouth. Repeat this 3 times.

After the last exhale, uncross everything.

Bring your hands together over your heart as if in prayer.

Take one more breath here, bow to your day's intention.

Stand tall and shake out your hands.

REFERENCES

Overcoming the
Mother Wound

Fincher, Susanne, The Mandala Workbook, Shambhala Publications, Inc,. Boston, MA, 2009

Hankes, Karla. Original visionary of the Gift of the Critical Mother Exercise.

Mehlomakulu, Carolyn, Creativity in Therapy. 20017 https://creativityintherapy.com/2017/04/tree-strength-art-directive/

Parnell, Laurel, A Therapist's Guide to EMDR Tools and Techniques for Successful Treatment, W.W. Norton and Company, New York, 2006

Science Daily, "At any skill level, making art reduces stress hormones." Drexel University, June 15, 2016. https://www.sciencedaily.com/releases/2016/06/160615134946.htm

Shapiro, Francine. EMDR Basic Principles and Protocols. The Guilford Press, New York, 2001.

Walker, Lauren, The Energy to Heal. Llewellyn Publications, Woodbury, MN, 2022.

ABOUT THE AUTHOR

VI

Overcoming the
Mother Wound

Mari Grande is a trained and licensed Art and Trauma therapist in private practice where she works with adults haunted by early childhood wounds.

www.marigrande.com

She also coaches and supports Individuals and Groups to Overcome emotional obstacles, and reconnect with themselves and others by using a variety of creative and energetic healing modalities.

www.creativehealingintegration.com

Notes

Notes

Notes

Notes

Notes

Notes

Notes

Notes

Notes

Notes

www.ingramcontent.com/pod-product-compliance
Lightning Source LLC
Chambersburg PA
CBHW082207070526
44585CB00020B/2323